Given in Memory of

Margaret Jones

by
Northport Women's Club

5-07

PUBLIC GARDENS OF MICHIGAN

Public Gardens of Michigan

by Miriam Easton Rutz

MICHIGAN STATE UNIVERSITY PRESS

East Lansing

Public Gardens of Michigan

by Miriam Easton Rutz

MICHIGAN STATE UNIVERSITY PRESS

East Lansing

∞ The paper used in this publication meets the minimum requirements of ANSI/NISO Z39.48-1992 (R 1997) (Permanence of Paper).

Michigan State University Press
East Lansing, Michigan 48823-5202

Printed and bound in Hong Kong, China.
07 06 05 04 03 02 1 2 3 4 5 6 7 8 9 10

        Library of Congress Cataloging-in-Publication Data
Rutz, Miriam Easton, 1943—
  Public gardens of Michigan / Miriam Easton-Rutz.
      p. cm.
Includes bibliographical references (p.   ).
  ISBN 0-87013-627-5 (cloth : alk. paper)
  1. Gardens—Michigan. 2. Gardens—Michigan—History. I. Title.
  SB466.U65 M47 2002
  712'.5'09774—dc21

Published with the generous support of
the Office of the Provost, Michigan State University

Cover and book design by Thomas Kachadurian

Cover Photograph: Fair Lane, Dearborn, Michigan, by Balthazar Korab

Back Cover Photograph: Cranbrook, Bloomfield Hills, Michigan, by Balthazar Korab

Uncredited photographs by Earl W. Rutz

Visit Michigan State University Press
on the World Wide Web at:
www.msupress.msu.edu

To Earl William Rutz,
my companion in the gardens and in life.

Contents

French Foundations 9

A Touch of Dutch 21

Aspects of England 31

Formal Fling 41

Rustic Revival 51

Nurturing Nature 61

Modern Movement 71

A Tapestry of Traditions 83

Appendices

    A Map to Michigan's Public Gardens 94

    A Table of Michigan's Public Gardens 95

    Garden Elements and Terms 97

Bibliography 101

Acknowledgments 106

Afterword 108

ABOVE: Slayton Arboretum, Hilsdale. Photo by Douglas Coon, courtesy of Hillsdale College.

OPPOSITE: Meadowbrook Hall, Rochester. Photo by Balthazar Korab

French Foundations

The grandiose Scott Fountain on Belle Isle, which is similar to the major fountains in the gardens of Versailles, is a reminder that the first European settlers in Michigan were French. Just as the French baroque style of gardening peaked in popularity in France at the beginning of the eighteenth century, Pierre d'Argenteuil, a French landscape gardener, traveled with Antoine de la Mothe Cadillac to help establish the settlement at Detroit. André Le Notre, the famous French landscape gardener, had recently created extensive gardens at Versailles for Louis the XIV. These formal gardens, with their wide-open spaces, spectacular fountains, rows of gleaming white sculpture, large bodies of water, and rectangular panels of lawn called *tapis verts*, represent the classic vision of French baroque gardens. Early drawings of the Detroit River settlement show a similar formal layout for the fort and gardens. Such formality suggests that d'Argenteuil was well-schooled in formal French baroque design and may have studied under Le Notre.

Formal French baroque garden design principles emerged out of a combination of ideas from both northern European medieval castle gardens and gardens of the Italian Renaissance. Medieval castle gardens took their formal design concepts from descriptions of fabulous Near Eastern Islamic gardens given by traveling minstrels and crusaders, as well as from biblical descriptions of the Garden of Eden. This garden of paradise was described in the Old Testament as a walled, square garden divided by four rivers with a tree in the middle and including every tree that was "pleasant to the sight." The reference in

ABOVE: **Scott Fountain at Belle Isle.** Photo by Balthazar Korab.

OPPOSITE: **A Michigan formal garden in the French tradition, Cranbrook House.**

BELOW: **A plan of French Detroit showing the King's Garden on the lower right.** Jacques-Nicolas Bellin, 1764. Courtesy of the Clements Library, University of Michigan.

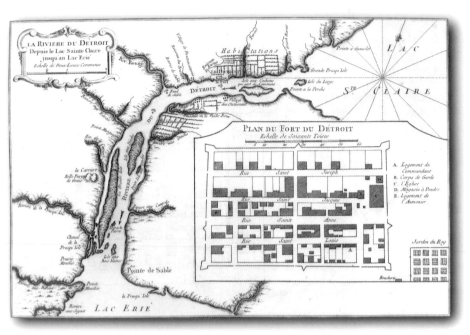

RIGHT: Terracing on steep terrain at the Villa d'Este, overlooking the countryside.

BELOW: The Cardinal's Table at Villa Lante shows bilateral symmetry.

the Old Testament to a "tree in the midst" of four rivers emerged in medieval garden design as a four-parts garden with a central feature, setting the groundwork for formal symmetry in garden design. Near East irrigation techniques, which moved water over flat landscapes in a grid pattern, also contributed to the use of geometric patterns in European garden design. Walled and gated medieval castle gardens included herbs, vegetables, flowers, fruit trees, and flowering trees. These gardens generally lay a distance from the castle, often across a moat, and were used primarily for pleasure. Craftsmanship, an essential component in these gardens, was expressed in the care given to details such as grass-covered seats, fountains, flowerbeds, latticework, arbors, and clipped shrubs. Over the course of time, castle gardens increased in size but maintained their formal four-parts symmetry and carefully crafted ornamental details.

Unlike French gardens, Italian renaissance gardens developed during the early fifteenth century as the villa rose to social and cultural prominence in the lives of wealthy Italians. The villa's house and garden, designed as an integrated architectural unit, overlooked the countryside. Formal gardens built on a series of terraces stepped down the hillside. Central sight lines tied balustrade-lined stone terraces together, and bisected the gardens into two matching halves rather than the classic four-parts divisions of medieval gardens. This design form, called bilateral symmetry, was a key concept in formal Italian gardens. Gravel walkways and low-cut evergreen hedges planted in patterns, called parterres, dominated these gardens. Water channeled from a nearby river tumbled through the gardens and was captured in powerful fountains, urns shooting jets of water, rushing cascades, and flat, tranquil sheets of water. Many of these design concepts originated in the writings of Pliny the Younger, who described in detail his family's villa near ancient Rome. The archaeological ruins of Hadrian's Villa outside of Rome stand as an example of the Roman gardens' inspiration for these fifteenth-century Italian gardens. Two of the finest Italian Renaissance gardens, Villa d' Este, also outside of Rome, and Villa Lante, near Tuscany, survived the centuries and are now open to the public. Both gardens have steep terraces, perfect bilateral symmetry, and beautiful water displays.

ABOVE: **Ruins of Hadrian's Villa, near Rome.**

BELOW: **A sight line focused on infinity, Versailles.**

After invading Italy in 1495, the French became enamored with the drama and precision of the terraced Italian Renaissance gardens. Later, François I, the French king, invited Italian artists and craftsmen to beautify his castle grounds at Amboise. During the sixteenth and seventeenth centuries other French nobles tried to build Italian-inspired gardens. It was impossible to carve impressive terraces or to create the great waterworks constructed at Villa d' Este and Villa Lante without steep terrain. Thus, French gardeners adapted Italian Renaissance gardens to the vast, even landscape of northern France. They built gardens with the same bilateral symmetry, balustrades, stone fountains, and geometric details, but included much longer sight lines focused on infinity through woodlands, and dredged massive canals and lakes into low wetlands. Fountains were even larger and more elaborate than those in Italy, but did not spray unless workers mechanically pumped water through them. The simple parterres on the terraces of

Parterres de broderies, **Versailles.**

Italian villas evolved into large, graceful, curvilinear and distinctly French patterns called *parterres de broderie*. These patterns reflected floral silk brocades, wallpapers, and ceramics popular among the French nobility.

Today, the most complete restoration of a sixteenth-century French garden can be seen at Villandry in the Loire Valley. Here, a magnificent restoration of three low-terrace gardens clearly shows the horticultural and agricultural divisions of a large castle domain. The uppermost terrace garden contains rows of square clipped trees, grape arbors, and an orchard. A large sheet of water called the mirror serves as a reservoir for irrigating the lower terraces. The middle terrace contains the formal pleasure garden. Flower-filled boxwood parterre panels represent aspects of love. Four of the panels show stages of love: tenderness, represented by hearts, flames, and masks; volatility by butterflies and fans; fickleness or follies by a labyrinth of hearts; and tragedy by sword and dagger blades. Below this parterre garden is a grand kitchen garden called a *potager*. This garden consists of nine large squares planted in geometric patterns, with different textures provided by a vast variety of herbs, fruits, and vegetables, with floral accents. Gravel paths lead to four rose-covered bowers marking the center of the *potager*. Subtle variations of greens and grays in the vegetable leaves, and bright colorful flowers, create an unforgettably beautiful picture. Espaliered fruit trees grow against sun-warmed walls. A low, wooden latticework fence, covered in vines, encloses the *potager*. Geometric patterns, like these at Villandry, can be seen in the gardens shown on maps of colonial French settlements in North America.

The gardens of Vaux le Vicomte, just northeast of Paris, are less well known and smaller than Versailles or Villandry. André Le Notre built the gardens at Vaux le Vicomte before he designed and oversaw the creation of Versailles. The chateau stands on a platform surrounded by moats, overlooking a gently sloping site cut by a central

Three views of Villandry.
BELOW: Flower-filled parterres with topiary. **BOTTOM:** Garden panels that show the stages of love. **LEFT:** Terrace gardens enclosed by vine-covered llattice fence.

axis. On either side of the central axis are *parterres de broderie*, matching water fountains, panels of lawn, statuary, and cross-axes. Le Notre designed Vaux le Vicomte for the financial minister of France, Nicholas Fouquet, who invited Louis XIV to a spectacular reception when the gardens were completed. Following the festivities, the king had Fouquet arrested and then hired Le Notre to design his own grounds. Most of the statuary, and even many of the trees were moved from Vaux le Vicomte to Versailles. Although Versailles is ten times larger and is the pinnacle of French baroque design, Vaux le Vicomte is the more precise and most well-maintained example of classical French gardening.

Louis Phelypeaux, the comte de Pontchartrain, was the French Colonial Minister of Marine in 1701. His position enabled him to fund a settlement at the site of present-day Detroit. Fort Pontchartrain du Detroit was named in his

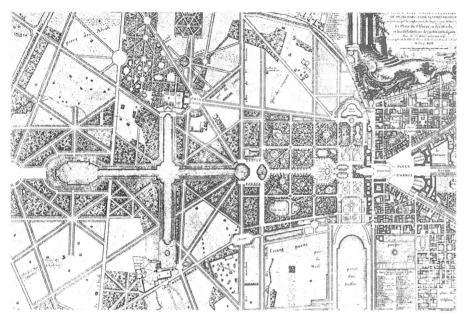

ABOVE: **A plan of the grand style of Versailles.**

BELOW: **Allée of trees with light on the trunks, Vaux le Vicomte.**

honor, and the inclusion of a landscape gardener in the settlement party reflected Pontchartrain's belief in the importance of gardens. During the seventeenth and eighteenth centuries, gardens were expressions of political power in the colonies as well as in Europe. This was especially so in France, and the grander the garden, the greater prestige an individual commanded in the court at Versailles. The Pontchartrain family integrated themselves into the ranks of the landed aristocracy at the court of Louis XIV through the purchase of a chateau outside of Paris. Pontchartrain hired Le Notre, one of his close friends, to redesign this residence in the grand style of Versailles. Le Notre spent his last days working on the design for Pontchartrain's estate, and many considered this garden to be his most perfect creation. Le Notre's etchings of his plans for Ponchartrain's gardens required moving mountains of earth, planting thousands of trees, and creating a long allée in the wooded area to the north of the chateau. An existing body of water was completely altered into a T-shaped canal surrounded by a grassy border similar to the Grand Canal at Versailles. These gardens and the impressive grand allée, lined with a double row of trees leading down the hill to the chateau, unfortunately no longer exist. A similar allée at Vaux le Vicomte suggests how stunning

Ponchartrain's allée must have looked when the light caught the trunks of the massive trees.

Le Notre had worked for seventy years in France, and d'Argenteuil, the landscape gardener sent with Cadillac to Fort Ponchartrain, was probably one of his many apprentices. Gardening in France in the eighteenth century was a much more comprehensive profession than gardening today. Experienced gardeners like Le Notre supervised the schooling of apprentices in horticulture, engineering, architecture, planning, and design. Sending gardeners to lay out new colonial towns, such as Montreal and Quebec, was a customary practice in French colonization efforts; old plans of these towns include garden details. Although maps and plans of Fort Ponchartrain show tree-lined boulevards and terraced gardens as well as a *jardin du roy*, or King's garden, we do not know if these plans were more than a vision. Nothing of the fort remains today and the site is now occupied by the Hotel Pontchartrain. We do know that travelers described neat flower gardens around houses, healthy orchards, and vineyards.

Formal French design regained popularity in postcolonial Michigan when President Thomas Jefferson sent Augustus Brevoort Woodward to the Michigan Territory as Chief Justice in 1805. He and Jefferson had been friends for over ten years, and it was through Jefferson that Woodward met Charles L'Enfant, the French engineer and architect who, with Jefferson, created a plan for Washington, D.C., based on French

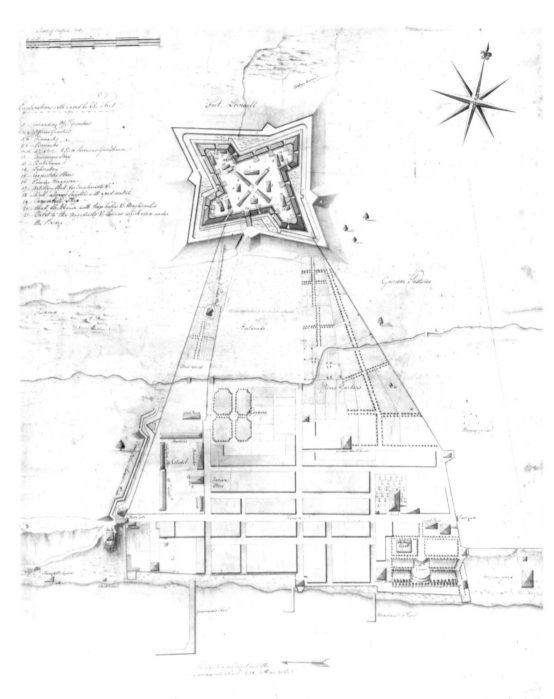

Map of Fort Detroit showing terraced gardens. John J. U. Rivardi, 1799. Courtesy of the Clements Library, University of Michigan.

ABOVE: City of Detroit, Grand Circus Park Renovations. Photo courtesy Albert Kahn Associates, Inc., Detroit.

BELOW: Plan for the streets of Detroit.

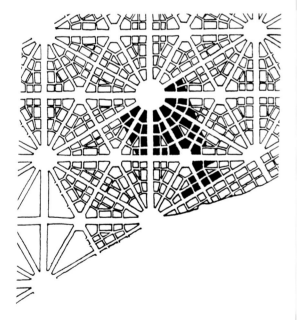

baroque principles. Woodward and Jefferson had been vitally interested in the plans for the new capital. Jefferson, an amateur landscape architect, had designed both his own home at Monticello as well as the University of Virginia. Enthralled by the dramatic sight lines of European gardens, Jefferson positioned the library at the University of Virginia to look west through the woodlands.

Woodward shared Jefferson's enthusiasm for French design and classical features, and the devastating Detroit fire of 1805 provided him with an opportunity to indulge his passion. Excited about the possibility of building a city without the problem of redeveloping over existing structures and roads, he sought to recreate a new Detroit, a city as beautiful as any found in Europe. Woodward created a design plan now called the Woodward Plan, using L' Enfant's plan for Washington, D.C., as a reference. The honeycombed street pattern he envisioned featured large green parks at the center of each octagon, connected by wide, tree-lined boulevards. He expected Detroit to grow to a city of two million inhabitants, but the Detroit citizens were doubtful and developers did not support his plan. Woodward only controlled development long enough to see the creation of one of the octagons, with its radiating streets and a central symmetrical green space, now called Grand Circus Park. Jefferson Avenue was built parallel with the river, connecting to Grand Circus Park by Woodward Avenue. Woodward Avenue thus formed a "T" with Jefferson Avenue and extended miles into the heart of Michigan, reminiscent of the extensive sight lines at Versailles. Grand River, Michigan, Monroe, and Gratiot Avenue are part of the octagonal street pattern, similar to a *patte d'oie* (goosefoot), which Le Notre used to organize space at Versailles. Grand Circus Park was redesigned to reflect the formality of French baroque gardens. Recent plans for Detroit reflect Woodward's dream for a beautiful city along European lines, calling for a linear park along the edge of the Detroit River that links the heart of the city with Belle Isle and the Scott Fountain.

Classical formal design dominated the teaching of landscape architecture in France for over three hundred years (1671-1968), but styles in America varied, and garden design in the nineteenth century was more reflective of the open, naturalistic English Landscape school of design. However, at the beginning of the twentieth century another rebirth of classical design, referred to as the beaux arts style, took place as

many American architects sought training at the École des Beaux Arts in Paris. The Scott Fountain, on Belle Isle in the Detroit River, competes in grandeur with any of the fountains and settings Le Notre created for Louis the XIV at Versailles. This majestic fountain was designed in the French baroque tradition in 1924-25 and is one of the finest examples of classical architecture in the United States. The fountain is made of white Vermont marble with 109 water outlets in the shape of human heads, dolphins, turtles, lions, and animal horns. The water cascades down a variety of levels, under the terrace and drive, to the lagoon thirty-eight feet

Views of Scott Fountain, Belle Isle.
ABOVE: The mosaic visable through the water. Photo by Balthazar Korab.
BELOW LEFT: Giant heads and fish pour water into the lagoons below. BELOW: Scott Fountain's shells and water jets.

below. Colorful tile mosaics lining the fountain sparkle through the water.

Architecture and garden designs from this period are often called neoclassical, focusing on the classical inspirations from French baroque design. Some of the same formal principals were also used in the 1924 plan created by T. Glenn Phillips for Michigan Agricultural College, now Michigan State University. The entrance at Abbott Road became a tree-lined boulevard leading to the central, green heart of the campus. The ceramic statue of Sparty, a university symbol, was placed on a sight line from the bridge off of the looped road over the Red Cedar River through the parade grounds to Demonstration Hall, creating bilateral symmetry. This plan helped to organize the growth of the campus.

The Horticulture Display Gardens, Michigan State University.
ABOVE: Geometric two-tone fountain at pivotal point. RIGHT: A sight line to the rose garden. OPPOSITE: Aerial view showing site line to the "Windows" sculpture.

Many gardens designed today incorporate formal elements such as sight lines, elaborate fountains, classical sculptures, and geometric precision. For example, in the 1990s these formal ideas resurfaced to organize the display in MSU's horticulture gardens. A major axis connects the statue of Liberty Hyde Bailey through a circular pool of water, the "Sunseed" sculpture, and a geometric fountain to the termination point at the "Windows" sculpture. This line is crossed by another line that leads visitors to the rose garden from the pergola. A two-tone granite fountain bubbles and cascades at the junction point of these axes. The continual reappearance of French formal design in Michigan gardens serves as a reminder of this region's early French heritage.

A Touch of Dutch

The Dutch, inspired by French and Italian garden designers, built fabulous gardens in Northern Europe during the same era as the colonization of New York. Structurally, Dutch gardens were similar to those in France, although they were smaller and usually contained within a wall and moat. Rows of trees, central points with radiating avenues, mazes, arbors, wooden fencing, topiary and low parterres filled with decorative flowers characterized these gardens. Water played a more modest role in Dutch gardens when compared with their French counterparts. Windmills pumped water from nearby reservoirs to create enough pressure to allow fountain jets to spray. The Dutch, more frequently than the French, placed sundials and statuary representing figures from Greek mythology in their gardens. Plants and flowers played a much greater role in Dutch, and subsequently, English garden design than in the more architectural French and Italian gardens. Colorful flowers both brightened planting beds and softened evergreen hedging. The art of cultivating flowers overshadowed formal design, and this art was probably the reason Dutch gardeners were sought after throughout Europe. The introduction of the tulip into the Netherlands from Turkish gardens in the seventeenth century transformed tulip cultivation into a national passion. The value of tulips skyrocketed, prompting tulipomania. During the craze, bulbs fetched such fabulous sums that rash speculators risked bankruptcy in the tulip markets.

The development of Dutch garden art reached its zenith just before William and Mary assumed the English throne in 1689. Known in the Netherlands as Stadtholder William III of the Royal House of Orange, William, along with his wife Mary, the eldest daughter of England's James II, directed the formation of splendid gardens at Het Loo, his palace near Amsterdam, with French gardeners trained under Le Notre. The marriage alliance between William and Mary resulted in similar design elements

ABOVE: **Tulips at the Veldheer tulip fields, Holland, Micihgan**

OPPOSITE: **A splendid resoration of the gardens at Het Loo, The Netherlands.**

Three views from Het Loo.
ABOVE: Sunken garden surrounded by trees. BELOW LEFT AND RIGHT: Berceau.

between the Dutch and English Tudor gardens. The restoration of some of William and Mary's gardens at Het Loo reveals the intimate spaces and precise design of seventeenth-century Dutch gardening. These gardens, redesigned in the popular English Landscape fashion when Napoleon's brother inhabited the palace, were restored to their original form based on contemporary accounts, records, paintings, drawings, and archaeological evidence. The restoration process revealed a series of sunken gardens with some similarities to Vaux le Vicomte, although much smaller and without a central axis. Surrounded by terraces, these sunken gardens contain stunning combinations of flower-filled parterres, pergolas, statues, fountains, cascades, vases, and topiaries. Queen Mary's private garden contains a lovely *berceau*. This intricate trellised walkway is covered with heavily pruned, fine-textured linden trees.

The larger Herrenhausen Garden, now a public park in the city of Hanover, Germany, is another restored formal garden built in a similar Dutch style. Founded in 1666 by Duke Johann Friedrick von Calenberg on an outlying estate, these gardens matured under the care of Sophie, spouse of Duke Ernst-August, between 1680 and 1692. Sophie spent her childhood in the Netherlands, and the Dutch style of the Herrenhausen Garden reflects this influence. She devoted herself to its expansion and care, making it the most beautiful and impressive garden of seventeenth-century

Germany. The Herrenhausen Garden is an expansive series of lawn panels and parterres, separated by gravel paths and lined with hedges and trees planted closely together and clipped into boxes. The Garden Theater features fifteen life-size gilded statues forming a kind of ballet emerging from behind paths lined with hornbeam.

English, Dutch, and French settlers transported these formal garden design principals to the east coast of the United States during the colonial period. The gardens at Williamsburg, the capital of Virginia from 1699 to 1781, were restored in the 1920s, preserving the Dutch and Tudor garden traditions loved by William and Mary. These gardens, at the Governor's Palace, were some of the grandest built in colonial America. The upper garden, directly behind the ballroom, cleaves on a central axis and consists of sixteen diamond-shaped parterres and twelve cylindrical topiaries. The lower garden's similar layout is brightly planted with red tulips. A *berceau*, planted with American beech, similar to the one at Het Loo, covers a long cross-axis with gazebos at each end. A maze, or labyrinth, modeled after the one at Hampton Court in England ranges beyond the north gate, and a canal-shaped lake lies nearby. Greenfield Village in Dearborn, Michigan, has a village green similar to the one in front of the Governor's Palace, featuring flower-filled parterres in front of the Martha-Mary Chapel.

Dutch colonists built beautiful agricultural estates along the banks of the Hudson River in upstate New York. The Vanderbilt mansion in Hyde Park, a National Historic Park in the Hudson River valley, is a legacy from early settlers. The mansion gardens illustrate how Dutch concepts such as the berceau and precision-planting were transferred to the New World. These early settlers had a major impact on landscape gardening in Michigan. In the 1820s, the commercial hub of the horticulture industry in America was Rochester, New York. First called the Flour City because of its export of wheat, Rochester soon became known as the Flower City. The ease in shipping on the Erie Canal lead to reduced market prices for farmers' crops. The glutted agricultural market made horticulture a viable business alternative. Soon, upstate nurserymen began to look for more land close to transportation but free from pollution and disease. The nursery trade spilled across Lake Erie into Monroe, Michigan. The French had farmed this rich agricultural region along the Detroit and Raisin Rivers since the early eighteenth century. Villages and roads established by the French gave New York

ABOVE: **Lawn panels and clipped trees, Herrenhausen Garden, Germany.**

BELOW: **Gardens at Vanderbilt Mansion, Hyde Park, New York.**

nurserymen the infrastructure and market base they needed to prosper. To expand their businesses, nurserymen encouraged new settlers to beautify their farms. Drawing on existing English, Dutch, and French garden design literature, nurserymen wrote books and magazine articles instructing homeowners in garden design.

In addition to the Dutch descendants who moved from New York into Michigan in the nineteenth century, Michigan has another more direct Dutch design connection. In the nineteenth century a group of Hollanders emigrated directly from the Netherlands to the west coast of Lake Michigan. One public landscape in Holland, Michigan, still exists as a reminder of this Dutch heritage—Centennial Park, originally the village market district. Here, Reverend A. C. Van Raalte, founder of Holland, created a traditional square similar to those in Europe. In 1876, Reverend H. Uiterwijk, responding to Michigan Governor J. Bagley's call for communities to plant "centennial trees," arranged for the planting of maple trees along the outside edge of the park. Symmetrical paths were mapped-out in gravel, and a "Liberty of Centennial" pole with stars and stripes was placed in the center, making the park a four-parts garden. Citizens planted trees and flowers throughout the park's interior. In 1902, Dutch immigrant Tenius Ten Houten donated a twenty-foot-high fountain made of tufa stone to replace the pole. This park has formal elements similar to those in the gardens at Het Loo. The

ABOVE: **Tufa stone fountain in Centennial Park, Holland, Michigan. RIGHT: Fountain at the center of the four-parts garden in Centennial Park, Holland, Michigan.**

picturesque fountain that crowns the raised center of the park sprays graceful arches of water out of dozens of concealed jets, creating a wonderfully misty atmosphere for the tiny plants that sprout in the fountain's rock crevices. Brightly-colored bedding flowers, planted in shapes that are cut into the lawn in the spring, thrive all summer. Dedicated caretakers have nurtured showy sub-tropical plants like palms, dwarf bananas, lantana, clivias, hibiscus, citrus trees, and fuchsia in the city's greenhouses, for placement in the park each summer.

Holland, Michigan, has other gardens designed for the display and sale of tulips. Built for commercial purpose, they are also extraordinarily beautiful. Windmill Island, just two miles from downtown Holland, has America's only working two-hundred-year-old Dutch windmill. The Posthouse Museum, a replica of a Dutch country inn, and other small shops, are set in a spacious lawn filled with over 100,000 tulips. Summer annuals bloom through autumn, drenching the island in color. The river setting, with its stately trees lining the water's edge, evokes the charm of the Netherlands' small towns. Dedicated to Dutch culture, this small garden displays beds of blooming perennials and annuals from June until October. Veldheer Tulip Gardens, part of a family-owned nursery, blaze with color in the spring when over two million tulips and other spring bulbs burst into bloom in the fields surrounding the demonstration gardens. The

ABOVE: **Veldheer Demonstration Gardens, Holland, Michigan.**

RIGHT: **A tiny corner park on Main Street, Holland, Michigan.**

Main Street of Holland is a garden in itself. Tiny corner parks provide settings for sculptures, flags, fountains, flowers, and seating. No other Michigan city boasts more flowers planted curbside or in plazas than Holland's downtown.

Other small gardens in Michigan exhibit the horticultural skills and design characteristics attributed to the Dutch. The Holmdene garden, on the campus of Saint Thomas Aquinas in Grand Rapids, is a tiny garden surrounded by a hedge. In this perfectly symmetrical space, flowers, shrubs, and statuary surround a central pool. A low, lawn terrace leads to the house, now an administrative office.

Dutch design elements characterize two other public gardens in the city park system in Lansing: the Cooley Gardens and the Francis Park Rose Garden. These gardens were built during the rustic revival in Michigan and have characteristics of many styles; but, because of their intimate scale and profuse use of flowers they are very reminiscent of Dutch gardens. The Cooley Gardens, once part of the most prestigious neighborhood in Lansing, are a delightful oasis hidden within the heart of the city near the Grand River. The Cooley Gardens share green space with the Scott House and the Cooley-Haze house, now the Michigan Women's Hall of Fame. Eugene Cooley bequeathed land for the Cooley Garden to the city in 1938 to be used for pleasure gardens. The dedication plaque on the pavilion states his intent—"A garden is nature's

TOP: **Coffee drinkers, Main Street, Holland, Michigan.**

ABOVE: **Central Pool, Holmdene Garden, St. Thomas Aquinas College, Grand Rapids, Michigan.**

BELOW: **Series of hedge gardens, Cooley Gardens, Lansing, Michigan.**

LEFT: **The sunken rose garden designed as a four-parts garden, Cooley Gardens, Lansing, Michigan.**

paradise." The gardens feature a series of formal, hedged garden rooms, each with an individual theme. The peony garden, the wildflower garden, the pavilion garden, and the rose garden all have colorful flowers arranged in well-kept flowerbeds. Tall evergreens hide the garden house. The sunken rose garden is designed as a four-parts garden. Here, rose bushes are mixed with bulbs, perennials, and annuals so that during the growing season the beds are always in bloom. The gardens in Francis Park have formal lines and colorful patterns. Throughout Michigan, small public spaces sometimes surrounded by walls or hedges, such as the prison gardens in Marquette, and embellished with flowers planted in colorful patterns, reflect the Dutch influence on Michigan's landscape.

ABOVE RIGHT: Colorful patterns, Francis Park, Lansing, Michigan.

RIGHT: Bilateral symmetry in the garden at Marquette Prison, Michigan.

OPPOSITE: Dutch influence, Dow Gardens, Midland, Michigan. Photo by Balthazar Korab

Aspects of England

The geometry and symmetry of French and Dutch gardens, with their classical sculpture and fountains, had fallen out of favor in England by the mid-eighteenth century. Romanticism influenced not only art and literature, but also garden design. Over the course of roughly fifty years, the English abandoned all architectural concepts and elements in their gardens. Designers now preferred naturalistic, idyllic landscapes of rolling pastures, serpentine rivers, and meandering pathways. Trees planted in clumps grew in natural forms, and flowers in the landscape were restricted to fields of daffodils and other naturalizing bulbs. The ha-ha wall, a retaining wall invisible from the house, allowed an unobstructed view of sheep and cattle grazing on undulating hillsides. Gothic ruins and classical temples placed on hilltops or around lakes, called follies, created scenes reminiscent of romantic landscape paintings. This purely landscaped style became known as the English Landscape school of design. Later, during the Victorian Era (1837-1901), landscape gardeners began to reintroduce classical elements, cutting flowerbeds into lawns to display colorful exotic plant material, and transforming landscape gardens into something more "gardenesque." This age of scientific discoveries, new technologies, forays into exotic lands in search of plants, and grand hothouses and conservatories, saw renewed attention to gardening as English taste in garden design spread throughout the world. Landscape architects and aficionados consider the Victorian Era as one of the great ages of gardening.

During this period, when gardening became popular among the masses, immigration from New York and New England had a major impact on landscape gardening in Michigan as the population of Michigan, particularly Detroit, expanded rapidly. A great many of the emigrants from New York and New England were well-educated, interested in garden design, and aware of garden books describing English Landscape

ABOVE: Natural idyllic landscapes, Stowe, England. Photo by Michael Hodges.

OPPOSITE: Recalling the English countryside at Grand Hotel, Mackinac Island. Photo by Balthazar Korab.

BELOW: Front lawn of manor house at Stourhead, showing the ha-ha wall.

traditions. Horticultural and agricultural societies sprang up across the state, and the Michigan Agricultural College was created for the purpose of teaching agriculture and landscape gardening.

Horticultural books by English garden authors were based on the history, topography, and climate of England, and thus their validity in America was sometimes questioned. One of the most influential British garden authors was Humphry Repton. His book, *Sketches and Hints on Landscape Gardening*, first published in 1795, outlined the perfect landscape garden by stating four points: The landscape should display natural forms and hide natural defects; it should be open, giving the appearance of "extent and freedom;" it should be designed in a naturalistic style, as if it were a "production of nature only;" "and all aspects of the landscape should be pleasing, and if not they should be concealed." This naturalistic theme was a constant, used by all English garden writers of the time. Repton compromised the idea of a strictly natural landscape, leading the way for later writers to propose the placement of more formal and exotic plants and architectural elements, into the landscape. As this trend continued, gardens became jumbles of flowerbeds full of ornamental pieces from around the world, a gardenesque variation of the English Landscape school. Ornaments, plants, and flowers dominated the garden obscuring the simple, smooth-flowing characteristic of the purely landscape style. Nurserymen promoted gardenesque landscape design in Michigan and elsewhere through books and journals.

Andrew Jackson Downing, a New York nurseryman and horticulturist, rephrased Repton's ideas in his book, *A Treatise on the Theory and Practice of Landscape Gardening as Adapted to North America* (1841). He was also the editor of the popular magazine, *The Horticulturist*, which promoted the "embellishment" of rural and suburban land." Downing simplified and codified contemporary gardening ideals into guidelines for creating well-designed gardens. He believed that the nature and location of the site itself should determine the choice of either "the beautiful" or the "picturesque" architectural or landscape style. Both styles were borrowed from English writers, and referred to naturalistic landscapes. The "beautiful" landscape was smooth and regular and included classical architecture, while the "picturesque" was dramatic, irregular, and punctuated by gothic architecture. Downing was also an eloquent spokesman for

Illustration of gardenesque in a public park in Bath, England.

LEFT: **Classical "Beautiful" style, Detroit Zoo.**

ABOVE: **Irregular planting and gothic architecture, Belle Isle, Michigan.**

BELOW: **Gothic "Picturesque" style at Woodmere Cemetery.**

the movement to create public parks and beautiful cities. At the time of his accidental death from drowning, he was designing an ambitious plan for the grounds of the U.S. Capitol, the White House, and the Smithsonian Institution in Washington, D.C.

Throughout Downing's career, he lauded horticulture's positive influence on society. In 1847 he wrote, "horticultural and its kindred arts, tend strongly to fix the habits, and elevate the character, of our whole rural population." Based on this belief, Downing supported the establishment of garden-like cemeteries to promote "moral elevation." The so-called "garden cemetery" movement began in the 1830s with the establishment of Mount Auburn cemetery outside of Boston, Laurel Hill in Philadelphia, and Greenwood in Brooklyn. Naturally beautiful sites along rivers or on wooded hillsides were purchased on the outskirts of growing urban areas. Such site selection became a distinguishing feature of cemeteries. The cemetery was further enhanced with carefully selected trees and shrubs planted along winding paths. Ornamental tombstones and monuments served as focal points, just as statues and temples graced the English landscape gardens. Designers often collaborated with local horticultural societies to develop arboretums in conjunction with cemeteries. The park-like atmosphere lured city-dwellers into these public spaces for picnics and relaxation.

The first city cemetery in Detroit, located between Gratiot and Clinton Street,

ABOVE: **Ornamental tombstones, Elmwood Cemetery, Detroit.**

BELOW: **Gently rolling hills, Elmwood Cemetery, Detroit.**

and extending a little east of St. Antoine Street, was purchased in 1827. It soon became a favorite Sunday resort. Silas Farmer, in *A History of Detroit and Wayne County and Early Michigan*, wrote, "being within easy walking distance, scores and hundreds of children and grown people, on pleasant Sabbaths, wandered about the grounds, reading and comparing tombstone inscriptions." In 1846, the cemetery was moved outside the city to a new site along Parent's Creek, formerly known as Bloody Run. Here in Elmwood Cemetery, the creek winding gracefully through the grounds provided a beautiful setting in gently rolling hills. Mature trees dotted the landscape, with other trees added in a random pattern. Gravestones and monuments completed the scene. A picturesque stone gate fronting Elmwood Avenue came later. Elmwood Cemetery was the epitome of a graceful English Landscape park, rivaling New York's Central Park in the beauty of its composition, in part because Central Park's designer, Frederick Law Olmsted, consulted on the project.

Olmsted was a leading landscape architect on the East Coast. He is acknowledged as the father of American landscape architecture, and his firm dominated the profession for over fifty years. He created parks to be available to all people, and he had high expectations for the visual and psychological effects of his designs. Olmsted believed that pastoral park scenery, like the English Landscape parks he had seen on his British travels, was a powerful antidote to the stress and artificiality of urban life. He drew inspiration for his designs from his travels, American natural scenery, and the writings of Downing and the English Landscape authors. Olmsted's reputation paved the way for his invitation to Michigan to advise on a plan for Belle Isle in the Detroit River. The public had used this island for recreation as early as 1845, when "the ladies" began to frequent it for picnics on Sundays. Olmsted sketched a romantic plan that used lagoons, meadows, and open space to enhance the natural landscape.

Almost all of the older communities in Michigan have cemeteries that were designed during the Victorian era. Gracefully laid out with mature trees, elaborate headstones, mausoleums, and entry gates, their similar names reflect the landscape chosen for their location. Evergreen, Mt. Hope, Woodmere, Oak Glen, Maple Dale, Beech Grove, Oak Hill, Greenwood, and Deepdale are virtual arboretums of majestic trees divided by serpentine pathways and decorative headstones. We think of parks as gently rolling landscapes with broad swaths of lawn and scattered trees, in large part because outdoor recreation and picnics took place in cemeteries before the public parks movement provided alternative grounds. Many parks all over the state reflect this pastoral heritage, whether recently built or maintained over the years. Belle Isle in Detroit, Ella Sharp Park in Jackson, Francis Park in Lansing, and Presque Isle Park in Marquette are just a few of these lovely spaces in the English Landscape style.

Another park-like setting with a debt to English design is the rolling, open green space at the heart of Michigan State University's East Lansing campus. The evolution of this space involved a great many people who shared

ABOVE: **Picturesque stone gate, Elmwood Cemetery, Detroit.**

BELOW: **Olmsted's rolling landscape in Central Park, New York City.**

BOTTOM: **Naturalistic Landscape, Belle Isle.**

ABOVE: Beal in the Garden, Michigan State University. Photo courtesy Michigan State University.

OPPOSITE: The campus of Michigan State University. Photo courtesy Michigan State University.

a love of landscape horticulture and garden design. The early founders of the Michigan Agricultural College set the original landscape style, which the north campus has followed to the present day. Gentleman farmer Bela Hubbard, originally from upstate New York, founded Michigan's first agricultural society in 1837. He wrote and delivered an address before the Michigan legislature in 1850 to encourage the formation of a state agricultural college. Titled "Memorial for a State Agricultural College in Michigan" this address stated that engineering, architecture, and landscape gardening should be taught and practiced in addition to agriculture. This is the first mention of teaching landscape gardening as a subject in an institute of higher education in the United States. The Michigan Agricultural College was founded five years later, and a course in landscape gardening was taught as early as 1863.

John Holmes, secretary of the Michigan State Agricultural Society, and professor of botany and horticulture at the college, was the moving force behind the selection of the property for the campus, a heavily wooded tract bordering the Red Cedar River. His appointment required him to inventory the trees, map the topographic features, and site the buildings for the early campus. Holmes placed the first college building near an oak opening on high ground, with native trees scattered picturesquely around the hall. The college's board minutes of 1857 resolved that "the grounds around the college premises be properly laid out and tastefully arranged." In the five years Holmes worked on campus, he did much to beautify the grounds and to give shape to the character of the campus. Asa Gray, from Arnold Arboretum at Harvard University, donated a large box of perennial herbs from the botanical garden in Cambridge, and florists and nurserymen of New York donated hardy plants, bulbs, and trees, which Holmes planted on the new campus.

Holmes was followed as professor of botany and horticulture and superintendent of the gardens by one of his students, Albert N. Prentiss. Prentiss was an alumnus of the college and taught the first required course in landscape gardening. He assigned the garden design books and articles written by Downing as well as a textbook by Edward Kemp, an English author: *How to Lay Out a Garden, Intended as a General Guide in Choosing, Forming, or Improving an Estate, with Reference to Both Design and Execution.* He also required students to draw plans in detail for areas of the campus,

Pond in Beal Gardens, Michigan State University. Photo by Balthazar Korab.

which he would then assess. Together, they used the campus as a laboratory and continued the landscape style, which the board had requested.

Professor W. J. Beal, who succeeded Prentiss, created the first botanical gardens in the Midwest. Beal Gardens remain open today and continue to reflect the English Landscape design principles. In 1884, the Department of Horticulture was separated from the Department of Botany, and Liberty Hyde Bailey, another graduate of the college, became professor of horticulture. Before coming back to Michigan, he had assisted Asa Gray and was exposed to the work of Frederick Law Olmsted in Boston. Bailey designed Eustace Hall and its adjacent garden as his teaching facility, and he wrote several books on garden design: *The Garden Lover; Garden Making: Suggestions for Utilizing of Homes Grounds; and A Manual of Gardening: A Practical Guide to Making of Home*

Grounds. Bailey articulated the design of the campus in flowery landscape terms in a report to the MAC board in 1885. He wrote:

> The grounds are laid out under the dominant features of the picturesque, and in the main, the individual objects are arranged with excellent taste. The preservation of natural undulations of surface, and of wooded banks and forest trees, with the entirely natural growth of spruces is especially fortunate. The grounds illustrate all the important principles of picturesque gardening.

Hidden Lake Garden, in Tipton's scenic Irish Hills, is another example of this picturesque garden variation. This arboretum is now owned by Michigan State University and displays thousand of trees, shrubs, and flowers in an English landscape setting. The original owner, Harry Fee, bought the land to farm, but soon realized that it would never be profitable. Instead, he planted trees and shrubs for aesthetic reasons. He built a greenhouse in 1926 and began to cultivate flowers. Fee wanted to make a series of naturalistic, beautiful, scenic pictures available to the public. Gently rolling hills, wildflower-dotted meadows, a serpentine lake, colorful summer flowerbeds, and a majestic conservatory all contribute to the Hidden Lake's picturesque quality.

The gardenesque variation of the English Landscape style is characterized most strongly by carpet bedding, and many gardens in Michigan reflect this influence. Carpet bedding consists of a pattern of dwarf or creeping foliage plants, especially colorful exotics, in flowerbeds. Early carpet beds used geometrical patterns, but after the success of some butterfly-shaped beds at an exhibit at the Crystal Palace in England in 1875 emblematic shapes were popular. Carpet bedding remained a staple of public park practice well after World War I in Michigan and the United States. There are examples of this in Centennial Park in Holland, as well as the carpet bedding at the State Capitol in Lansing. Two long, linear beds flank the entry walkway to the Capitol and exhibit a different floral pattern each year. The surrounding lawn, dotted with large trees planted in groups and gently sweeping away from the Capitol, was inspired by English Landscape design. This combination of naturalistic landscape and formal design is found in many Michigan gardens.

BELOW: **Hidden Lake Garden, Tipton, Michigan.** Photo by Balthazar Korab.

BOTTOM: **Carpet bedding at the State Capitol Square, Lansing.**

Formal Fling

As the nineteenth century drew to a close, two opposing garden styles rose in popularity in Michigan. Both were revivals of older ideas: one was a rebirth of the formal, while the other was a return to nature. Increasing numbers of wealthy Americans traveling abroad fueled the desire for formal gardens at home. Impressed by the lavish estates of Italian and French nobility, they sought landscape gardeners capable of creating elaborate plans like those seen on their travels. At the same time, more American design students began to study at the École des Beaux Arts in Paris. This famous French school of fine arts had continued to dominate the teaching of garden architecture in France since the seventeenth century. Students from the Beaux Arts school returned to the United States trained in the principles of Greek and Roman classical architecture. The ideas most emulated in these beaux arts gardens were those seen in Italian villas and French chateaux. The garden's central and all-important theme was composition, of which the principal elements were balance (in the form of bilateral symmetry), repetition of elements in a regular pattern, and unity of all elements into harmonious whole. The rebirth of classical, formal garden styles occurred all across America, but especially near Detroit where private fortunes amassed in the auto industry funded the creation of estate gardens.

In this same period, garden design became a profession. Many landscape gardeners joined the American Society of Landscape Architects (ASLA) after it was formed in 1899. The original ASLA members had no common background in their training. They had studied civil engineering, natural or applied science, business, and philosophy. The only woman founder, Beatrix Jones Farrand, had received private instruction in botany, horticulture, and landscape gardening at the Arnold Arboretum under the tutelage of Asa Gray. The term "landscape architect" dates from 1857, when Frederick

ABOVE: Beaux arts design, Biltmore House and gardens, Ashland, North Carolina.

OPPOSITE: View toward the west terrace, Crankbrook House. Photo by Balthazar Korab.

BELOW: Mall at Central Park, New York City. Designed by Frederick Olmsted.

Law Olmsted first used the term while designing New York City's Central Park in 1857. With the formation of the ASLA most professional garden designers began to adopt the title of landscape architect, as opposed to landscape gardener, even though they essentially did the same kind of work: designing parks, cemeteries, and estates. The new society considered its profession as a fine art related to architecture, and embraced the beaux arts principles.

The rebirth of the formal style of design first received national attention at the 1893 World's Fair in Chicago, known as the World's Columbian Exposition. Olmsted selected the site, completely renovating the landscape park he had previously designed. The Columbian Exposition was conceived as a grand urban park commemorating the four-hundredth anniversary of the discovery of the New World. Olmsted drew on European ideas from the École des Beaux Arts to lay out a formal design with a strong central axis and cross axis. A large canal, similar to the one at Versailles, created a central open space lined with classical buildings sporting decorative columns and domes. The fairgrounds contained sculptures, urns, and fountains. This exposition, known as the White City, featured bold designs and details reminiscent of Hadrian's Villa. The impressive and beautiful form of this carefully designed ideal city ushered in the "city beautiful" movement in America. Fair visitors returned to their own cities determined to make improvements. Michigan, just a train ride away, had large numbers of people who visited the fair and who brought back artifacts to place in the public spaces and private gardens in Michigan.

The World's Columbian Exposition was just one of the many pathways through which people learned about formal garden design. Literature was another. In 1894, Charles Platt, an etcher, painter, and architect from New York City, published the first illustrated book in English on Italian Renaissance gardens, titled *Italian Gardens*. He also designed a series of estates in Grosse Pointe; thus, his work is strongly tied to Michigan. He introduced the idea of designing the house and garden as a unit, organized around a series of outdoor rooms. His book was followed ten years later by Edith Wharton's beautifully illustrated, *Italian Villas and Their Gardens*, (1904). The colorful illustrations featured pictures of balustrades, terraces, fountains, and vistas. Mariana Griswold Van Rensselaer, a refined New York lady of Dutch ancestry, wrote *Art Out of*

The Grand Camal at Versailles, Central-axis.

Doors, which influenced the city beautification movement. She received a gold medal for distinction in literature from the American Academy of Arts and Letters in 1923, which recognized her as "a champion of good taste and common sense in the arts." Many magazines published at the turn of the century focused on garden design and landscape as a fine art. Beatrix Farrand eloquently expressed the art of landscape gardening when she wrote, "With this grand art of mine I do not envy the greatest painter, or sculptor or poet that lived. It seems to me that all arts are combined in this."

In the early twentieth century, institutes of higher education began to offer curricula in landscape architecture. These institutions influenced garden design via teaching and writing. Henry Hubbard, a professor at Harvard University, and Theodora Kimball, the librarian for the Harvard design school, wrote a book together titled *An Introduction to the Study of Landscape Design* (1917). Kimball was also the editor of

View over the rose garden and Lake St. Clair from Alger House, Detroit.

Landscape Architecture, the magazine of the ASLA. Their book was enormously popular with landscape architecture professors and students at Michigan Agricultural College and the University of Michigan. It reflected the thinking of landscape architects such as Olmsted and Charles Platt, and discussed in detail how to design estate grounds—at the time, the most common work for landscape architects.

Hubbard and Kimball stressed that the location and orientation of the house should be determined primarily by the factors of "access, light, view and topography." They believed that the house, forecourt (carriage turn), and terrace should be treated as an architectural unit with additional buildings, a service area, fields for sports and games, and large open areas incorporated into the design. The open space would give a sense of freedom, and from this area the smaller elements of the estate design would be accessible. The enclosed and protected gardens, visible from the house, would serve as additional outdoor living rooms. They felt that the dominance of the estate house required a formal treatment of the landscape, as well as, the "practical fact that fences, shelters, and flower beds are more readily made and managed in formal shapes." Additional structures, tied to the house architecturally with pergolas or walls, formed interesting visual points providing comfortable resting places "to enjoy a view or watch a game of tennis." Outdoor recreation areas included horseshoe pits, croquet courts, lawn tennis courts, outdoor swimming pools, space for garden theaters, and sometimes large areas for polo or golf.

Many of the landscape design concepts outlined in Hubbard and Kimball's now-classic work can be found in estates built in Michigan prior to the depression. The Alger House in Grosse Pointe, Applewood in Flint, Cranbrook House in Bloomfield Hills, Meadow Brook Hall in Rochester, the Fisher Mansion in Detroit, and the homes of both Henry and Edsel Ford near Detroit all contain elements of formal design. In each case, terraces and forecourts act as extensions of the architecture, and large, green, open spaces organize additional structures and facilities for outdoor sports. Formally designed terraces near these houses contain symmetrically placed statuary and fountains. All of the gardens feature spectacular views overlooking a river or a lake, and naturalistic landscapes envelope the formal gardens, giving the design a feeling of spaciousness.

The work of Charles Platt and Ellen Shipman, an East Coast design team, can be seen today at the Grosse Pointe War Memorial Center. Built in 1910 on Lake Shore Road for Russell A. Alger, the son of General Alger, the house and gardens were designed as a unit. Located on one of the highest elevations along the Michigan shoreline, the Alger house overlooks Lake Saint Clair. A lawn panel called the "bowling green" still stands between the house and the lake. The lakeside façade of the house features an Italian loggia, or porch, and pergola that face a formal garden of roses and perennials. A view through a wrought iron gate near the entry reveals a courtyard with a sculpture standing in a pool of water. This courtyard, flanked by carefully pruned parterres and beautiful weeping cherry trees, is one of the most perfect formal gardens in Michigan.

Applewood, in the center of Flint, stems from Charles Stewart Mott's desire to

ABOVE: Lawn terrace extending from Cranbrook house.

BELOW: View of parterred terrace through gate, Alger House.

ABOVE: **Allée of crabapple trees, Applewood, Flint.**

RIGHT: **Lawn panel with wellhead, Applewood, Flint.**

live on a "farm in the city," surrounded by beautiful gardens. William Pitkin, a landscape architect and Mott's cousin from New York, created the original landscape plans. Mott made many decisions about plant selection and placement, and he took daily inspection walks with his Scottish gardener. As Mott became more involved in philanthropy, he donated most of the property to Flint Junior College, later renamed Mott Community College. His wife, Ruth Rawlings Mott, decided to preserve Applewood in 1977 as a memorial to her husband, and commissioned a plan to preserve the original design for the grounds while making them accessible to the general public. The long linear house focuses on two formally designed terrace gardens. The living area looks out on one terrace with a pool and fountain set in a manicured lawn. The other terrace contains a wellhead that Mott brought back from Florence, Italy. The wellhead sits in the middle of a lawn panel and is surrounded by perennial borders that are contained by carefully clipped hedging. To the west of the house, down the slope, is the original farm garden, which has been redesigned to contain a collection of daylilies, rhododendrons, and shade-loving perennials. Two rows of flowering crabapple trees divided by a gravel walk form a European-style allée. These demonstration gardens contain herbs, wildflowers, a water lily pool, ornamental grasses, a rock garden, and vintage non-hybrid vegetables like those grown in the 1920s.

French and Italian formal gardens provide the inspiration for the extensive gardens surrounding Cranbrook House. Construction of the house and gardens began in 1904 and continued to evolve through the 1920s. George Gough Booth, publisher of the *Detroit News*, and his family, continually redesigned and expanded their gardens. Each time they traveled to Europe they brought back artifacts to place in their gardens. The most interesting are Roman columns, which frame the view to the lake. A long sight line extends from the west terrace of the house and directs the eye to the entry pavilion of the art museum, part of the Education Complex. A rectilinear basin of water at the foot of the terrace is reminiscent of the canals in French baroque gardens. The east side of the house is a complex of terraced gardens featuring a variety of focal points and formal flower gardens. Matching lions, urns, and vases accentuate the bilateral symmetry apparent throughout the gardens. In the woods, further from the house, a cascade of water ripples through shell-shaped pools before falling into a small stream. This design element originated at Villa Lante and other Italian villas. Although not as spectacular at the one in Herrenhausen, a Greek-style theater built in 1915 adds to the garden's classical character.

Alger House, Applewood, and Cranbrook House are not the only twentieth-century gardens featuring formal elements. Meadowbrook Hall, an enormous, baronial mansion inspired by a sixteenth-century Tudor manor house, is now part of the Oakland University campus. The gardens were built by Matilda Dodge, the widow of John Dodge, who loved flowers and formal gardens. She had plans to surround the mansion with gardens, but only completed a portion of her vision. These gardens were linked to the house with an axis focusing on a Marshall Frederick sculpture. Intimate gardens stretch around the Fisher Mansion, and a long linear pool of water with jets, as well as symmetrical allées, still exist. This is now the Bhaktivedanta Center; lotus ponds and peacocks have been added to the original design.

The gardens at both Fair Lane, Henry Ford's house, and the Edsel and Eleanor Ford House are a mix of formal and rustic styles. Fair Lane is surrounded by four formal gardens: a tea garden enclosed by a hedge, with a spectacular entry gate and

TOP: Columns brought from Rome flank the staircase leading to Cranbrook House.

ABOVE: Sight line art museum, Cranbrook.

TOP: Concentric circles in rose garden, Edsel and Eleanor Ford House.

ABOVE: Set of linear pools cutting through garden at Fisher Mansion.

pavilion; a flower garden in blue tones; a perennial garden; and a terrace that juts out toward an open space, allowing for a view of the rising sun. The formal gardens at the Edsel and Eleanor Ford house are a distance from the house, organized along a sight line beginning with the tennis court. The line cuts through a small rose garden, designed in a series of concentric circles around a small pool, and continues on to a formal garden. This simple panel of lawn contains a rectangular reflecting pool at the center and walkways around the outer border. Circles of stone mark the corners of the paths, and the far end terminates in a half-circle trellis of wood and chain around a circular bed of flowers.

In addition to these once-private estates, formal design elements exist in numerous publicly-funded spaces in Michigan. On Belle Isle, for example, the gorgeous Scott Fountain, which has been restored to its original grandeur, lies with its accompanying formal gardens in front of the Whitcomb Conservatory. Likewise, the Horace Rackham Memorial Fountain graces the spacious mall at the Detroit Zoological Gardens. Approximately twenty tons of bronze was used to cast the bears, turtles, frogs, and life-size seals sitting in the white marble basin, surrounded by a balustrade. The fountain was commissioned by Rackham's widow and presented to the zoo in 1939 to commemorate his role as the first president of the zoological commission. Sparks Park in Jackson, another example, is home to a gigantic cascade that was lovingly created for the community by Sparks after he had seen similar cascades in European gardens. A sight line is still visible through the wooded park, looking east from the top of the cascade.

The renewed interest in classical formality resulted in the creation of new formal gardens across Michigan and the addition of classical elements or entire gardens in existing English Landscape gardens. Most public gardens in Michigan contain some formal elements, an axis, an allée, an arcade, or a terrace with sight lines that run toward a piece of sculpture. In part, this return to classical design was fueled by modern design styles inspired by the industrial revolution and its accompanying new technologies. At the same time rustic and natural designs competed with, and were incorporated into, formal garden designs. The growing interest in nature, a response to both modernism and the rebirth of a more formal style, paved the way for the growth of the state park system.

TOP: **Formal gardens, Whitcomb Conservatory.**

ABOVE CENTER: **Rackham Fountain, Detroit Zoo.**

ABOVE: **Arbor with bilateral symmetry, Francis Park, Lansing, Michigan.**

LEFT: **Gigantic cascade in Sparks Park, Jackson, Michigan.** Photo by Balthazar Korab

BELOW: **Sight line through the woods, Sparks Park, Jackson, Michigan.**

Rustic Revival

A rustic revival took place alongside the rebirth of formal design in the early twentieth century. Increasing mass production and industrialization during the Victorian Era sparked renewed interest in nature and craftsmanship. The Arts and Crafts Exhibition Society, founded in England in 1888, embraced a philosophy that valued nature and craftsmanship. The Arts and Crafts movement, as this philosophy was called, attracted a large following throughout the United States from the 1890s to 1920s. Inspired by nostalgia for European craft guilds of the Middle Ages and the idealization of a romanticized, bygone rural society, this movement also drew on the increasing popularity of Japanese arts and crafts. Gardens inspired by the Arts and Crafts movement contain an eclectic mix of design styles with a particular emphasis on rustic elements.

While often found blended with formal gardens, these rustic gardens had a more intimate, personal character. Formal gardens with their crisp lines, bold classical architectural elements, and statuary imported from Europe, were intended to impress. Rustic gardens were intended to be comfortable and private. While often sharing a similar formal layout, classical statuary, or formally shaped hedging, rustic gardens featured naturalized plant materials that softened formal layouts. Intimate spaces, detailed craftsmanship, and natural appeal reflected the ideals of the Arts and Crafts movement. Flowers played a more important role in rustic gardens than in the manicured evergreen formal gardens. Carefully trained flowering vines climbed over arbors and lazily cascaded onto houses and garden structures.

Herbaceous borders contained well-planned mixes of perennials, which bloomed from early spring until late fall. Although appearing casual, they required a great deal of planning and maintenance. Natural-appearing meadows and pools of water added to the rustic feel of these gardens. Walls, terraces, gazebos, benches, and walks constructed

OPPOSITE: Naturalized plant materials soften formal layouts, Meadowbrook Hall, Rochester.

BELOW: Carefully trained vines, Alger House, Detroit.

ABOVE: **Wooden arbor, Fernwood.**

RIGHT: **Gazebo constructed from local fieldstone, Slayton Arboretum.**

from local fieldstone harmonized with surrounding terrain. Wooden arbors, gates, and fences carefully crafted from rough-hewn timbers accented the rustic look. Adirondack-style furniture and Japanese design elements often accented the garden. The appeal of these gardens extended beyond the exquisite estates of the elite and spilled into both modest private gardens and public spaces.

Gertrude Jeykll, an English garden designer, wrote many books and articles about landscape gardening that were read in America during this period. The growing popularity of gardening as a hobby for middle-class people, particularly women, supported her career as a garden writer and designer. She collaborated with Edwin Lutyens on some of the greatest houses and gardens of the Arts and Crafts period in England. Of all her contributions to garden design, the one most often cited is her inventive use of color in herbaceous borders. Inspired by what she saw in cottage-garden borders, she refined herbaceous borders into a calculated art form. She constructed her borders, set in garden rooms backed by evergreen hedges, with a thoughtfully mixed palette of hardy perennials, biennials, bulbs, and tuberous plants. A master at balancing color and texture, she clustered single plant materials into elongated teardrop drifts that overlapped and intertwined. Two large, linear herbaceous borders flanking each side of the Capitol in Lansing are reproductions of the ideas described in Jekyll's *Colour Schemes for the Flower Garden*. A movement of color flows from reds and oranges to yellows, creams and corals, then to lavenders and blues. White and silver gray are used for accents. Rustic herbaceous borders set within formal layouts or landscape gardens such as these emphasized the naturalizing of plant materials.

The incorporation of rustic elements into formal garden design was most fully realized in Britain where the Arts and Crafts movement had begun. Hidcote Manor Garden in Gloucestershire, England, designed by the owner, is one lovely example. An offset walkway runs through the garden flanked by yew hedges and pleached

ABOVE: Rainbow colors in herbaceous beds flanking the Capitol, Lansing, Michigan.

BELOW: Herbaceous borders and carpet bedding on Michigan State Capitol Square, Lansing.

Two views of Hidcote. TOP: Doorway cut into a hedge for an intimate entry. ABOVE: Circular pool filling the entire garden space, Red Garden.

Two views of Dumbarton Oaks. BELOW: Formal gardens designed by Beatrix Farrand. BOTTOM: Lovers' lane pool.

hornbeams, the trunks of which suggest a colonnade. A series of hedged garden rooms lead away from the main walk, each with an individual character. Plant materials suggest architectural elements. Doorways, cut through hedges provide an intimate entry into some of the gardens. The variety in character and style of each garden room reflects the eclectic nature of Arts-and-Crafts-period garden design. In one garden room a circular pool fills the whole enclosure, another is planted with all-white herbaceous borders, and a third features plantings in shades of red. Gates frame pretty views over the countryside. Bowers, arbors, and other nooks and crannies create a private feel. The intimate spaces, flowering herbaceous borders, and eclectic ornamentation spread among many private garden rooms form a large, coherent composition with a rustic character.

Beatrix Farrand, a well-known East Coast landscape architect, created similar gardens in the United States. Following the work of Jekyll, Farrand approached garden design with subtle and harmonious colors, a softness of line and an unobtrusive asymmetry. Her most memorable garden is Dumbarton Oaks in Georgetown, near Washington, D.C., designed with both formal and rustic elements. Farrand created garden rooms, like those seen at Hidcote, tied together by axes and walkways. Walled terraces near the house, with clipped hedges, geometric patterns, and classical sculptures, reflect the formal character of the Georgian manor. Orchards, secluded seats, meandering walks, and informal groupings of trees lead away from these formal hedges into a naturalistic landscape garden that contains an oval pool, called the Lover's Lane pool, and a rustic amphitheater made of bricks and lawn. Flowery herbaceous perennial borders line many walkways, particularly Melisande's Allée, a naturalistic walkway that forms the base of the fountain terrace. Careful detailing of wrought iron balconies, interrupted by the natural texture of ivy trained in a strong horizontal line, and the well-crafted flagstone used on the Arbor Terrace, reflect Arts and Crafts design elements.

Many estates in Michigan that are now public gardens incorporate rustic and naturalistic elements into formal and landscape gardens. Cranbrook Education Complex is a manifestation of George Booth's lifelong interest in architecture and the crafts, and reflects his dedication to the philosophy of the Arts and Crafts movement. Booth wanted to integrate art into daily life. The gardens at his home, Cranbrook

House, have a strong rustic character but include many formal design elements brought back from his travels in Italy; thus, they reflect both beaux arts design and the Arts and Crafts movement. Herbaceous borders on either side of the rectilinear pool of water on the west terrace contain a wonderful mix of perennials in loose, irregular groupings. Rough, stone walls and flagstone steps, used to create the terraces, soften and naturalize the formality of the terraces. A naturalized slope of daffodils and stepping-stone paths through the woods further add to the rustic qualities of this estate garden.

Cranbrook House.

Other Michigan estates such as Applewood, Meadowbrook Hall, the Kellogg House on Gull Lake, the Cottage at Fernwood, Fair Lane, and the Edsel and Eleanor Ford House, contain gardens that reflect qualities similar to those seen at Hidcote, Dumbarton Oaks, and Cranbrook. For the most part, the architects copied from the English Tudor manor houses, reflecting the medieval inspirations of the Arts and Crafts movement. Small garden rooms, linked together with walkways and designed using bilateral symmetry, are filled with herbaceous borders, intimate spaces, and elements crafted from rough, natural materials or Japanese characteristics. For example, the hedged, rose garden at Fair Lane contains a wrought iron teahouse having a circular door and a roof with an oriental slope. This garden focuses on a central, square lily pond with an elk sculpture placed in the center. Gorgeous iron gates at the garden's entrance frame the view of the pond and its elk. The blue garden, featuring linear hedged beds of perennials planted in strictly blues, is similar in its the thematic use of color to gardens at Hidcote. In a more naturalized section of the gardens, a grotto memorializing Ford's friend John Burroughs nestles into pines and ferns. Stepping-stones through the alpine rock garden lead wanderers to a rustic bridge, crossing a small cascade and surrounded by native plants.

Through her writing and social activities, Louisa Yeomans King helped spread the use of rustic garden elements beyond estate gardens into more modest private

Rustic fountain backed by a naturalized slope at Grand Hotel, Mackinac Island.

gardens and public spaces. King's writings introduced Jekyll's rustic style and carefully crafted herbaceous borders to American middle-class gardeners. Gertrude Jekyll even wrote the foreword to one of King's books, *The Flower Garden Day by Day*, which King then dedicated to Jekyll. King lived and worked in Alma, Michigan, for twenty-five years. She moved with her husband and three children to Alma in 1902, where she helped establish the Garden Club of Michigan in 1912 and was the club's first president. She helped organize a civic improvement league and sponsored an annual flower show at her home, Orchard House. Her garden at Orchard House no longer exists, but the organization she founded, the Garden Club of America, still promotes civic beautification. King inspired women to participate on committees for civic beautification. These committees then planted beautiful herbaceous borders at parks, train stations, and public buildings—a practice community organizations continue to this day.

The grounds around the Grand Hotel on Mackinac Island are reflective of a more eclectic, public, rustic landscape style. They have been redesigned many times, but the picturesque setting overlooking the straits—the lawn sweeping below the hotel—suggests the ambiance of an English estate. The slope in front of the hotel is naturalized with native wild flowers, particularly colorful in the fall. Hedges and fences divide the garden into smaller, separated spaces. Exquisite classical and rustic ornamental elements reflect the eclectic nature of the Arts and Crafts period. Beautifully crafted white benches create a stunning repetitive pattern along a walk. The Bocca della Verita Fountain and the crying Zeus statue, which were imported from Italy, are nestled into an evergreen woods near the entry to Cranbrook House. Such a variety of styles within garden spaces are common to public parks of this period. Remnants of these parks remain today.

Japan inspired another element of Arts-and-Crafts-period gardens. The Japanese approached gardens philosophically, carefully incorporating symbolism and design. Arts and Crafts garden designers borrowed Japanese elements to create Japanese-styled garden rooms, but without the symbolism intrinsic to Japanese gardens. Many people were first exposed to the art and export products of Japan at various World's Fairs, particularly the 1893 World's Colombian Exposition, which featured a half-scale reconstruction of the Phoenix Hall of the Byodo-in Temple at Uji, near Kyoto in Japan. This exotic structure provided an impressive example of a traditional Japanese timber-frame building. Likewise, San Francisco's 1894 Midwinter Fair featured a stunning Japanese Tea Garden, which introduced Americans to East Asian garden design. Garden designers incorporated details copied from Japanese gardens such as fences, gates, bridges, lanterns, rocks, waterfalls, raked sand, lakes, and stepping-stones.

Japanese influence further punctuated the rustic character and intimate spaces of Arts and Crafts movement inspired gardens. In Michigan, Japanese-styled garden rooms were incorporated into other, larger gardens. The Whitcomb Conservatory on Belle Isle, Cranbrook House, the Lewis Arboretum on the Michigan State University campus, Tokushima Friendship Garden at Rust Park in Saginaw, and the tiny garden in the Fernwood Botanical Gardens in Niles, all have Japanese-styled

TOP: Native wildflowers on the slope in front of Grand Hotel, Mackinac Island.

ABOVE: Fencing and repetitive benches dividing space at Grand Hotel, Mackinac Island.

BELOW: Bocca della Verita Fountain enclosed by evergreens.

gardens. Carefully selected plant materials give them a Japanese character, and Japanese-inspired garden ornaments provide focal points. Paths wind over and around a rock-edged pond at Cranbrook and lead through a gate to view a lantern reflected in the water. Graceful, arched bridges span the lake. The Lewis Arboretum garden features a Japanese-landscaped garden as well as a Zen dry garden, which consists of raked sand and a few carefully placed stones. This small Zen garden is enclosed on all sides and has a viewing platform. Tokushima Friendship Garden, comprised of a teahouse and garden, was established as a symbol of friendship and cultural exchange with Saginaw's Sister City, Tokushima, Japan. The teahouse is authentic in design and crafted in keeping with traditional Japanese architecture. The tiny Zen dry garden at Fernwood consists of raked gravel, groupings of rocks, and evergreen plant material surrounded by a fence and a hemlock hedge.

The Arts and Crafts movement, centered in upstate New York, inspired a rustic revival in garden design and introduced into the American landscape well-crafted, small, naturalistic gardens based on both European medieval gardens and Japanese gardens. A Midwestern variant of the Arts and Crafts movement called the Prairie school of design developed in Chicago in the early twentieth century. Michigan, located between the center of the American Arts and Crafts movement in upstate New York, and the center of the Prairie school in Chicago, is home to a rich assortment of estate gardens and parks systems initiated by these philosophical and architectural movements.

ABOVE: **Zen dry garden, Lewis Arboretum, Michigan State University.**

OPPOSITE: **Arch bridge, Cranbrook.** Photo by Balthazar Korab.

BELOW: **Tokushima Friendship Garden.**

Nurturing Nature

The Arts and Crafts movement fostered a strong effort to preserve native landscapes. Landscape architects of the Prairie school, a Midwestern variant of the Arts and Crafts movement, translated Arts and Crafts philosophies into designs for vast public parks. This design style captured the soul of the Midwestern landscape with its low, gentle contours, and spectacular rockwork and waterfalls, suggestive of the ravines and bluffs found along Lake Michigan. Jens Jensen, Genevieve Gillette, and O. C. Simonds were central to the push for environmental preservation in the Midwest, particularly in Michigan.

Jens Jensen emigrated from Denmark to America in 1884, where he settled in Chicago and went to work for the West Chicago Park District. In 1906, he became the park districts superintendent and chief landscape architect. In this position, Jensen reshaped many of the parks into his own naturalistic style. Jensen was active with the loosely-knit band of writers, artists, architects, and landscape architects who called themselves the Prairie school. His parks in Chicago were the first public expression of the prairie spirit on the landscape. Jensen founded the Clearing, his "school of the soil," located on the bluffs of the Door Peninsula overlooking Green Bay in northern Wisconsin. Here he stressed his ideas for creating natural designs and preserving native landscapes. He also formed an organization, called the Friends of the Native Landscape, which helped to create state park systems in Illinois and Michigan.

Genevieve Gillette, a 1920 graduate of Michigan Agricultural College in landscape gardening, worked in his office. She gained valuable experience helping him organize events for the Friends of the Native Landscape. With her help, the organization successfully lobbied for a state park system in Illinois in the early 1920s. She had become such a skilled and ardent advocate for the preservation of native landscapes that Jensen urged her to return to Michigan to help in the creation of a state park

ABOVE: Genevieve Gillette Visitors' Center, Hoffmaster State Park, Michigan.

BELOW: Reconstructed prairie at Fernwood Botanical Center near Niles, Micihgan.

BOTTOM: Nature trail around a lake at Hidden Lake Gardens near Tipton, Michigan.

system there. Collaborating with P. J. Hoffmaster, who had been hired as the state conservation director, and working with an organization she founded, Michigan Parks Association, Gillette lobbied the Michigan legislature to protect sand dunes, trillium fields, white pine forests, and wetlands. Her first effort was through the Friends of the Native Landscape organization. She organized a meeting attended by Jensen and other Illinois members at a stunningly beautiful natural site near Ludington. Gillette invited influential Michigan people to attend this meeting in order to explain to them the group's work. Her efforts resulted in the creation of Ludington State Park. In her later life, she was instrumental in securing Sleeping Bear Dunes and Pictured Rocks as National Lake Shores. She helped establish a number of other state parks, including Hartwick Pines, and P. J. Hoffmaster State Park where there is a visitor center named in her honor. All of these parks have nature trails meandering through wetlands, forests, and fields of wildflowers. It is fortunate for the state that Gillette saw all nature as a garden and was able to convince the legislature of this important concept.

State park nature areas require design, but not in the sense of a designed garden. Trails lead visitors through the landscape, minimizing destruction yet bringing people and nature closer together. Michigan's state parks integrate public access with natural preserves through carefully designed trails and picnicking sites. The popularity of nature trails extends beyond the state park system.

Many of the public gardens in Michigan today include nature trails that wander through wetlands and prairies. Fernwood Botanical Gardens and Nature Center, near Niles, has extensive trails along the river and on through a reconstructed prairie. Wetland trails with boardwalks allow visitors to walk over water at the Frederik Meijer Gardens in Grand Rapids. Hidden Lakes Gardens, near Tipton, features numerous trails throughout the arboretum. Universities and small colleges in Michigan also include nature trails on their campuses. A wildflower garden at The Matthaei Botanical Gardens at the

LEFT: Modern sculpture in grasses, Matthaei Botanical Gardens.

ABOVE: Wetlands, Slayton Arboretum, Hillsdale College Campus.

BELOW: Frostic studio emerging from the wetlands near Benzonia, Michigan.

University of Michigan juxtaposes plants that originally grew wild in the southern Great Lakes region with modern sculptures. Here, seven miles of hiking trails loop through multiple habitats. Hillsdale College, in southeast Michigan, is home to the Slayton Arboretum, where trails wind through extensive wetlands. The artist, Gwen Frostic, built her studio into the wetlands near Benzonia and made nature her garden.

Some of the private estates in Michigan reflect this naturalized design style. Henry Ford was enamored with the philosophy of the Arts and Crafts movement. While his house at Fair Lane resembled a Scottish Baronial castle perched above the Rouge River, the house was supposed to blend with the natural landscape. When finished, however, it dominated the landscape like a fortified castle, seeming doubly awkward by looking as if it were sliding down the hill. Ford hired Jens Jensen, the Chicago landscape architect, to suggest ways to improve the grounds and take advantage of views up and down the river. Jensen advised making some minor changes in the grade to solve these problems. Ford, who wanted gardens to go with the house, asked Jensen to undertake Fair Lane's landscaping. Ford also hoped to establish a hydroelectric plant on the Rouge River. Jensen carefully sited the dam into the river's landscape.

ABOVE: House at Fair Lane, taking advantage of views up and down the river.

BELOW: Rockwork over the dam, Fair Lane.

Spectacular rockwork gave the dam the appearance of natural rapids. He created a great meadow with a slight bend in its length, leading to a small lake. The meadow is set at such an axis that during the summer the early morning sun softly highlights the trees, and in the evening the sun sets at the end of the meadow. Jensen also created gardens at the Edsel and Eleanor Ford House. Here he designed another great meadow with rockwork around a naturalized pool for swimming. Both of these gardens would have lacked any formal garden elements except for the demands of Clara and Eleanor Ford, who insisted on formal rose gardens and terraces.

In addition to Jensen and Gillette, Ossian Cole Simonds, another important Midwestern landscape architect, worked in Michigan to preserve and create natural landscapes. Simonds created many cemeteries, parks, residences, and subdivisions throughout the Midwest. He always tried to maintain the essential qualities of the native landscape. Born in Grand Rapids, he studied engineering and architecture at the University of Michigan and intended to practice architecture. After working on Graceland Cemetery in Chicago with Jensen, he shifted careers to landscape architecture. Simonds was instrumental in establishing the University of Michigan's landscape architecture program. He emphasized the need for studying nature as an inspiration for design. Nichols Arboretum in Ann Arbor is a prime example of his work. As the Arboretum has aged, it has grown more beautiful. His design works perfectly with the natural contours of the site, providing a wonderful landscape for wandering, and majestic views both of meadows and of the Huron River.

Simonds also consulted on Michigan Agricultural College, securing forever the natural quality of the north campus. He was hired in 1913 to make recommendations to the board for the development of campus. His greatest influence was his designation of all the ground included within an area he marked on a map by a dotted red line as "a sacred space," from which all buildings must forever be excluded. He explained:

> . . . this area contains beautifully rolling land with a pleasing arrangement of groups of trees, many of which have developed into fine specimens. This area is, I am sure, that feature of the College which is most pleasantly and affectionately remember by the students after they leave their Alma Mater and I doubt if any instruction given has a greater effect upon their lives.

Titus Glen Phillips, the first student to graduate with the landscape gardening option from Michigan Agricultural College, also appreciated this sacred space. Hired by the campus in 1924, he developed a plan to preserve and enhance the romantic, picturesque character of the grounds. Phillips enlarged the sacred space, and his plan has been used as a general framework for campus expansion, protecting the integrity of the central landscaped park.

TOP: **Rockwork connecting swimming pool to lagoon at Edsel and Eleanor Ford House.**

ABOVE: **Native landscape at Nichols Arboretum, Ann Arbor, Michigan.**

ABOVE: Panoramic view with exhibits separated by a ha-ha wall, Detroit Zoo.

BELOW: One of Shurtleff's drawings for the Detroit Zoo.

The Zoological Park in Detroit, conceived in 1911 by the Detroit Zoological Society, is a wonderful mix of competing garden design styles popular at the beginning of the twentieth century. The idea for the naturalistic quality of the exhibits came from the work of the Hagenbeck family, wild animal trainers who had built a zoo without bars in Hamburg, Germany. The landscape had been carefully crafted in such a way that the animals were separated from the visitors by moats and a ha-ha wall. They also created sight lines that allowed for panoramic views of more than one animal display at a time. The Hamburg Zoo became world famous, and the Detroit Zoological Society wanted a similar plan. In 1916, Arthur Shurtleff, a Boston landscape architect who had worked in Frederick Law Olmsted's office and had designed the zoo in Prospect Park in Boston, was hired to draw a plan for the Detroit Zoological Society. This plan combined the traditional, formal style used for zoo designs in American cities with a series of natural-looking barless exhibits similar to those in the Hamburg zoo. These barless exhibits surrounded a mall lined with animal

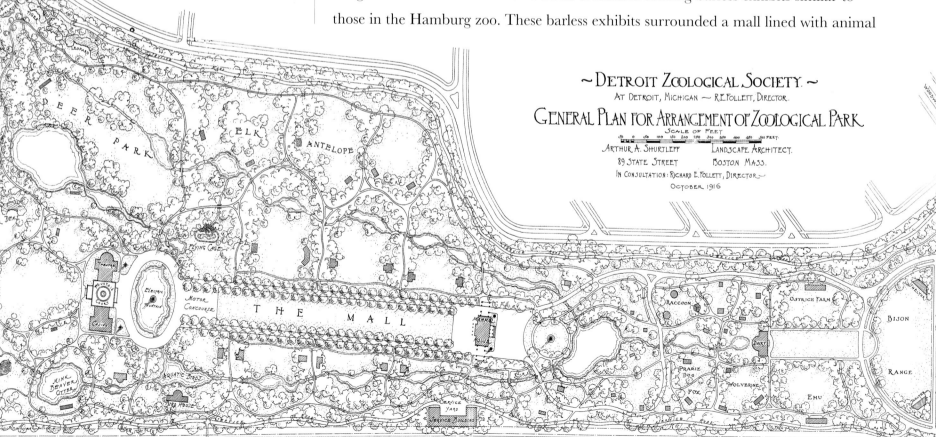

~ DETROIT ZOOLOGICAL SOCIETY ~

AT DETROIT, MICHIGAN ~ R.E.FOLLETT, DIRECTOR.

GENERAL PLAN FOR ARRANGEMENT OF ZOOLOGICAL PARK

SCALE OF FEET

ARTHUR A. SHURTLEFF   LANDSCAPE ARCHITECT.

89 STATE STREET   BOSTON MASS.

IN CONSULTATION: RICHARD E. FOLLETT, DIRECTOR

OCTOBER 1916

houses. The design incorporated winding paths through existing trees, as well as two large lakes dredged into existing drainage channels. These picturesque lakes allowed for panoramic views of other animal exhibits. Over a ten-year period, Shurtleff drew three detailed variations of the plan for the Zoological Society that show an evolution from an extremely formal plan to a predominantly naturalistic plan featuring more barless exhibits than buildings. Work on the site began even before he had completed the

final drawings. The cave-like bear display, separated from visitors by a moat, was the first barless exhibit, built in 1928. The formal sight line down the mall over the lake to this exhibit anchored the Zoo's design.

Over the years, the zoo has followed the basic master plan created by Shurtleff, even though the Hagebecks were retained in 1929 after Shurtleff's departure. Animal exhibits, buildings, and sculpture displays were added, especially by the WPA during the New Deal. Michigan-made Pewabic tiles, products of the Arts and Crafts movement, provide beautifully detailed accents to zoo

TOP: **Pewabic tiles viewed through water, Scott Fountain, Belle Isle.**

ABOVE: *Trabejo rustico*: **rustic bridge over the trout pond, created by Dionicio Rodriguez, Detroit Zoo.**

BELOW: **Similar style bridge in McCourtie Park, Somerset Township.**

buildings. These tiles can also be seen in the base of the Scott Fountain in Belle Isle. The concrete bridge over the trout pond, sculpted to look like tree branches, is one of the Zoo's more curious details. Similarly modeled concrete tree branches ornament the old chimpanzee house. This form of sculpture is a type of Mexican rustic folk art, *el trabejo rustico*, or rustic work, which combines two artistic traditions: Mexican folk art and American rustic. Dionicio Rodriguez, the best-known of the itinerant artists who traveled from commission to commission during the Great Depression, signed his name on the trout pond bridge. This type of sculpture blended well with the natural parks constructed in Michigan during the Great Depression.

Two other parks that display *el trabejo rustico* structures are in southeast Michigan. McCourtie Park in Somerset Township, contains a series of folk art cement sculptures executed by an artist affiliated with Rodriguez between 1930 and 1933.

These structures were constructed from wet cement to resemble dead tree trunks, complete with decayed branches and patches of missing bark. The most elaborate works of art are seventeen bridges that cross the meandering Goose Creek and its tributary at regular intervals. The replications are so precise that the timber components display insect damage, peeling bark and patches of lichen. The bridges vary in size and complexity, and no two are exactly alike. This is the largest concentration of Mexican rustic folk art in the Midwest. The Slayton Arboretum on the Hillsdale College campus displays two gazebos crafted from stone and cement to look like rustic structures in naturalistic settings. One overlooks a lush meadow and the other sits atop a constructed alpine mountain, complete with a rushing stream. A walk in the wetlands reveals yet another bridge.

The Arts and Crafts movement sparked both a formal, yet rustic revival, and a naturalistic, yet well-crafted and designed revival of earlier landscape styles. Preservation of earlier styles was the impetus for Henry Ford's Greenfield Village, which features gardens in a rustic style at the Cotswolds Cottage and Susquehanna Plantation. Public interest in the natural landscape inspired the creation of many of the finest public gardens in Michigan and fostered the state park movement. New Deal public works programs provided labor and funds to create public parks using native materials. As a result of these merging forces, Michigan's state and national parks attract thousands of tourists every year.

ABOVE: **Wet Cement formed to resemble a dead tree at McCourtie Park.**

BELOW: *El Trabejo rustico* **bridge over wetlands in Slayton Arboretum.**

OPPOSITE: **Rock wall, dovecote, and Cotswold cottage, Greenfield Village, Dearborn, Michigan.**

Modern Movement

Industrial factories in Michigan, particularly those in Detroit, set a new form of garden design into motion during the early twentieth century. The efficiency of Michigan's highly industrialized automobile factories had a profound influence on modern design styles. Assembly lines required precise, repetitive, fluid motions similar to the patterns seen in new artistic styles. Modern design, which went by many different names in Europe, represented motion and the machine age. Modern designers streamlined existing neoclassical forms and further united the garden with modern architecture. Asymmetrical and sensuous geometric shapes took their form from the function for which the spaces were designed. Functionalism, as this design philosophy is often called, favored extreme simplification of garden design and eliminated the use of a wide variety of plant materials and flowers. While the Arts and Crafts movement had been a reaction against the machine and a return to the natural, the modern style reversed this trend.

Modernism, with all its ambiguity and variations, was an international movement whose design manifestation is often referred to as the International Style. In Europe, modern design ideas came together at the World Exhibition in Paris in 1900. The term Art Nouveau, or Moderne, came from France, Jugendstil from Germany, Sezession from Austria, and Karelianism from Finland. Later, the Bauhaus School in Germany simplified these ideas even further. What these schools had in common was the desire to create a sense of unity in all art forms, which included architecture, interior design, and landscape architecture. Modernism was a simplified, holistic approach to design.

While many garden designers shunned modernism and continued designing in the beaux arts tradition or used elements from the Arts and Crafts movement, modern

OPPOSITE: Cranbrook. Photo by Balthazar Korab.

BELOW: Frank Lloyd Wright designed home, Oak Park, Illinios.

ABOVE: Motion motif gate pattern at art museum, Cranbrook.

BELOW: Finnish Pavilion.

garden designers blazed into the future hand-in-hand with architects. Often they were trained as architects rather than as landscape designers. New garden makers sought to reinvent nature with their own imagination. Nature provided curvilinear motifs and sensuous lines that characterize the modern style, while the machine age gave the motifs their motion. In design, the natural world was abstracted beyond recognition. This change began in Europe, but incorporated Japanese art principles of unity, composition, and structure into new modern art forms. The modern movement had a profound effect on architecture and gardens in Michigan, with perhaps the greatest input for change coming from Finland via an architect named Eliel Saarinen.

Saarinen, a world-renowned master of environmental arts, was born in Finland during the transition from Russian control to Finnish independence. National romanticism created a revival of the arts called Karelianism, a term that came from the Finnish national epic, the Kalevala, a mystical legend from the oral tradition about the founding of Finnish culture. Artists and intellects roamed Finnish forests in search of their cultural roots. This quest for a national identity spawned an unmistakably Finnish art style. Saarinen, with his weighty, sentimental, solidly imposing design style characterized by distinctive contours and simple ornamentation, won the competition to design the Finnish pavilion at the Paris World Exhibition in 1900. The pavilion's free use of traditional motifs became a demonstration of Finland's independent spirit. Its powerful design gained an international following for Finnish architecture. Saarinen immigrated to America in 1922 and was appointed visiting professor of architecture at the University of Michigan. One of his students, Henry Booth, introduced Saarinen to his father, George Booth, who commissioned Saarinen to help plan the Cranbrook Academy of Art campus. Booth collaborated with Saarinen, transforming the school and its grounds into a stunning plan where sunlight fell onto sculptures enclosed in courtyards, with vistas framed by nature. Saarinen coordinated wall colors, furnishings,

architectural details, proportions, massings of plants, paths, gates, gardens, and lights into a harmonious, comprehensive, modern design plan.

Saarinen moved to Cranbrook and produced several master plans for the Cranbrook Educational Complex. Booth often initiated projects with very detailed sketches of what he wanted, and Saarinen then developed the sketches into mature, architectural expressions. Saarinen took Booth's Arts-and-Crafts-inspired concepts one step further, integrating them with emerging principles of modernism. Saarinen also refused to reject industrialization for the sake of handcrafts. The art museum and library complex, completed under Saarinen's direction in 1942, is a dramatic integration of architecture and landscape. A covered, colonnaded walk connects the library and museum, framing vistas of the reflecting pools and the gardens beyond. The Triton Pool Court and the Orpheus Fountain unite with the building both architecturally and

ABOVE: Orpheus Fountain, Cranbrook.
Photo by Balthazar Korab.

BELOW: Covered colonnade, Cranbrook.

ABOVE: **Patterns on pavement.**
ABOVE RIGHT: **Benches reflect the pattern, Cranbrook.**

BELOW: **Wright house in Oak Park, Illinois.**

BOTTOM: **Windows and doors open on to terraces, May House, Grand Rapids, Michigan.**

spatially. A cross-axis moves from the lightly spraying Orpheus Fountain through the colonnade to a rectilinear set of cascading ponds. These tree-lined ponds, which spill water into the Triton Pool, feature a varied set of figures. The pattern in the pavement around the pool and court matches patterns of interior design details. This geometric pattern on the pavement travels up the walls and into the museum and library. The benches in the courtyard have a similar form, making the garden an extension of the architecture. Plants are used like building materials: hedges make walls, lawn serves as carpet, and trees provide a ceiling. The landscape and the architecture work together in a wonderful example of the principles of the modern garden.

Chicago architect Louis H. Sullivan coined the phase "form follows function." Although the majority of the architecture at the World Colombian Exposition in 1893 had been in the beaux arts tradition, he had used the new modern style for the transportation building. Sullivan's designs prepared the groundwork for the career of Frank Lloyd Wright, the leader in the new modern school of architecture. Wright set up his office in Oak Park, west of Chicago, and houses he built in the neighborhood clearly show his transition from his Victoria-Era roots to the modern style of architecture. He is still the most famous architect in America, and his buildings look as modern in form today at they did in the 1900s.

His first large commission in Michigan was the Meyer and Sophie Amberg May House in Grand Rapids, in 1909. The two-story residence emphasized the horizontal quality of the Michigan landscape. The windows and doors open out onto terraces stepping down into the garden. Walls and planters, incorporated into the architecture with boxed hedges, complete the architectural lines. The building has an intrinsic relationship with the landscape. The interior and exterior spaces intermingle, making the garden a part of the architecture. The same geometric shapes found inside the

Interior and exterior spaces mingle, Meyer May House, Grand Rapids, Michigan.

house, on windowpanes, and woven into the carpets and drapes, appear outside in the garden. A large painting of stylized hollyhocks reflects the garden outside. The house dominates the site, but the garden it features shows Wright's landscaping skills.

Michigan's own native architect and son of the founder of the Dow Chemical Company, Alden B. Dow, apprenticed with Wright in the summer of 1933. The following year, Dow built his own studio in the park-like Dow Gardens that his father had created in Midland. The asymmetrical studio wanders through carefully selected vegetation along a controlled stream, uniting architecture with landscape architecture. In the

Asymmetrical studio blending in with landscape, Dow Gardens. Photo by Balthazar Korab.

1970s, Alden Dow transformed the arboretum, which his father had established at the turn of the century, into a unique blend of the ideas from the Prairie school of design, Japanese gardens, and modernism. Dow added Japanese elements and color into an undulating landscape of rolling lawn. The stream, which winds its way throughout the garden, impounds itself into several ponds, and ripples over waterfalls and rock formations in an elegant way reminiscent of Japanese gardens. Lawns beckon visitors off the paths to focus their eyes over the landscape toward such views as that of a red, arched bridge or an azalea reflected in the water. There are a number of modern sculpture pieces hidden away in secret gardens, but elements of the Arts and Crafts movement are also found in the garden. The stream, reflecting a combination of modernism and naturalistic styles, flows toward the greenhouse, passing gnarled tree roots and arbors with cascading vines along the way.

ABOVE LEFT: **Azalea reflected in pond.**
ABOVE: **Elk, Dow Gardens.**

BELOW: **Hart Plaza, Detroit.**

The simplification of the landscape during the modern movement resulted in gardens as streamlined as freeways and shopping malls. The most popular exhibition at the 1939 World's Fair in Flushing Meadows, New York, "The World of Tomorrow," in the General Motors Pavilion, featured an enormous model of a gleaming and efficient City of the Future. Efficiency and low maintenance, particularly in public spaces, became the most important concept for public gardens. Some of the spaces created at this time can hardly be called gardens. An extreme example is the Hart Plaza, which was created by Isamu Noguchi, a sculptor, architect, and landscape architect. This space, on the Detroit River, is a termination park for Woodward Avenue. The whole plaza is a concrete sculpture with small niches for plants. A monumental abstract aluminum and steel sculpture rises above a bubbling, circular fountain, spraying water from its ring in computerized configurations. The fountain represents the power of the Motor City and provides a visual focus for pedestrians. A spacious amphitheater near the fountain attracts crowds for summer festivals, but most of the year it remains a huge, empty concrete space.

Minoru Yamasaki, another modern architect, created the master plan for Wayne State University Campus in Detroit. The campus, composed of a series of buildings along the existing street grid, became a compact urban campus consisting of internal pedestrian courts linking low buildings with many interesting small gardens. He designed the McGregor Memorial Conference Center overlooking a sunken garden and reflecting pool. The building and garden flow together and the unity reflects the serenity of the Japanese Zen garden. The reflective, still body of water contains bridges, which allow visitors to walk over the pool. Water comprises the majority of the garden,

ABOVE: Water garden, McGregor Memorial Conference Center, Wayne State University.

BELOW: Rectangular lakes, General Motors Technical Center. Photo by Balthazar Korab.

with a few reeds, iris, and azaleas, contrasting with the travertine marble.

During the same period, Eliel and Eero Saarinen designed the General Motors Technical Center, in Warren. This complex was patterned after Cranbrook, but with a completely different architectural look. The long, low, minimal structures of metal and glass were arranged around open courtyard spaces so that each set of buildings related closely to the outdoor gardens. The most dramatic element is the central twenty-two-acre rectangular lake, which all of the buildings face. Blocks of plantings, lawn, buildings, and the lake, which includes rectilinear islands placed in asymmetrical patterns, create a grid pattern reminiscent of a Mondrian painting. Thomas Church, a landscape architect from California, whose work was well-known in Michigan from the articles he wrote in *Sunset Magazine*, as well as his book, *Gardens are for People*, designed the garden to showcase the Technical Center.

Church's influence across the country was considerable. Born in Boston, he grew up in the San Francisco Bay area and studied landscape architecture at the University of California, Berkeley, and at Harvard University during a time when both schools were breaking away from beaux arts design concepts. The social and economic conditions of the Great Depression allowed him to develop a new, cost-efficient mode of garden design. He treated the garden as an outdoor living room with extensive areas of paving. To reduce maintenance costs he used mowing strips, ground covers, and clipped evergreen hedges, retaining existing trees as sculptural counterpoints. He traveled to Finland to study design and when he returned he incorporated new dynamic, asymmetric, curved forms into his abstract designs, embracing nature with his forms. His design style was a perfect complement to Saarinen's architectural plans for the Technical Center.

In the 1960s and 1970s, Michigan cities continued to look to Church for design inspiration. Landscape architecture programs at Michigan State University and the University of Michigan saw professors teaching the California style of modern landscape architecture. Designers from the West Coast were invited to Michigan to work. The California style of design incorporated a great deal of concrete. This style has not worked well in Michigan because freezing and thawing destroys the pavement rapidly. In addition, maintaining Michigan's winter-hardy plants in little spaces has been nearly impossible. An example of this design style was the large public landscape created along the riverfront in Flint in the 1960s. The project, which called for large concrete fountains, retaining walls, and intimate seating areas, had to be modified extensively for safety and maintenance. Lansing's new government complex, designed and built in the 1960s, also reflects this streamlined concrete style. A simple series of flat planes of lawn, concrete, and brick with trees planted in a grid over a parking structure compose the design. This public space was designed for ease of care, but the controversy over its design has fostered many discussions over the identity of public space and the subsequent role of gardens in cities.

There was not enough money to finish the futuristic design for the government complex; and the highly ornamental capitol, dating from the Victorian Era, was not torn down as originally planned. In the 1980s, a move toward preservation of public buildings and gardens gained momentum. A Lansing-based group, Friends of the

The designs of Thomas Church.
ABOVE: Sensuous concrete form reclining in a swimming pool. Photo by Michael Laurie. **BELOW: Asymmetrical curved forms.** Photo by Michael Laurie.

ABOVE: **Capitol complex, Lansing, Michigan.** Photo by Balthazar Korab.

OPPOSITE: **Sight line leading to west façade of Capitol.** Photo by Balthazar Korab.

Capitol, mounted a campaign to preserve and restore the capitol building as well as the grounds. Their efforts resulted in an international award-winning restoration project. The complementing landscape plan called for a return to the original setting created for the building. Trees obscuring the base of the building were cut away, and a ribbon of trees was planted near the street, allowing the building to dominate the site as originally conceived. Carpet bedding, the planting of colorful annuals in precise patterns popular during the Victorian Era, lines both sides of the entry walk. Herbaceous borders sweep across the front lawn at the base of the building. The capitol and grounds now stand in their original grandeur.

The renewed interest in historical preservation that supported the capitol restoration has fostered an appreciation of gardens in public landscapes and a renewed interest by the general public in visiting gardens full of flowers. Newly constructed gardens and renovations in older gardens reflect a revival of historical forms that do not adhere to a single style. Even modern gardens increasingly incorporate colorful flowerbeds into their sparse designs. Recent tendencies to blend garden design traditions have resulted in varying styles for newly created gardens in Michigan. In their ability to incorporate many historic design elements, these gardens simultaneously reflect Michigan's diverse garden heritages, but resemble none.

A Tapestry of Traditions

Gardens built at the turn of the twenty-first century exhibit no unified style. Instead, they display a tendency to incorporate many different ideas and styles from earlier Michigan gardens. These gardens often accompany postmodern architecture. Postmodernism, as it relates to art, architecture, and landscape design, is a reaction against the simplification and abstract ideas of the modern school of design. Postmodern gardens use contemporary materials common to modern gardens, such as concrete and steel, but they tend to incorporate more ornamentation, color, and plant material than modern gardens. Citizens are again more involved with public gardens, and participate in community design decisions. As early as the 1960s, many cities and towns cleaned up their riverfronts, creating parks and bike trails along these former industrial wastelands. They beautified main streets by preserving historic building façades, and adding trees and flowers. Citizens continue to help plant trees and build small parks; they line streets with miles-long banks of flowers to create beautiful entries into their cities; they protect historic sites; and, they insist on more public art. Private estates, which are now public gardens, have prepared management plans that make gardens accessible to the public while retaining the historic intent of the original design. Most of Michigan's universities and colleges have enhanced their campuses, preserving historic elements and adding promenades, fountains, sculptures, and flowers. Corporations continue the tradition, set by General Motors, of surrounding their head-quarters with gardens.

Ideas for garden design still come from Europe. Gardens in Paris, built in the last few decades, have all the power and majesty of Versailles, although the lines of the gardens are asymmetrical, and details combine a mixture of historic elements and care-fully crafted garden spaces. The Parc de Bercy, built on a cleared industrial site, rejects

OPPOSITE: Postmodern elements mix with colorful plantings at Children's Garden, Michigan State University. Photo by Balthazar Korab.

BELOW: Sports arena covered in lawn at Parc de Bercy, Paris.

ABOVE RIGHT: Streamlined curves blend with rustic elements, Parc de Bercy, Paris.

ABOVE: Streetcar tracks alongside vegetable gardens, Parc de Bercy, Paris.

Three views of Getty Center Garden, Los Angeles. ABOVE: Labyrinth surrounded by water. ABOVE RIGHT: Intimate space contrasting with bold architecture. RIGHT: Water rushing down a rocky chute.

modern architecture to the extent that the sports arena is almost entirely covered in grass. This structure anchors the long, linear park linking several neighborhoods together. Graceful bridges arch over streets, making it possible for pedestrians to stroll the entire length of the park without encountering motor vehicles. The urban gardens intertwine with an historic pub, and include streetcar tracks, public vegetable gardens, and rose gardens. Streamlined curves blend with rustic elements. Flowers are planted in both formal and informal groupings. Pools of water, surrounded by naturalized plant materials, reflect the architecture of surrounding buildings and sky. This successful park has attracted an abundance of new housing developments along its borders.

Postmodern gardens at the Getty Center in Los Angeles exhibit many of the same design ideas. Historic features are mixed with sleek design forms and intimate spaces contrast with the bold architecture. The central feature is a medieval labyrinth surrounded with water and ringed with vegetables, herbs, and flowers similar to the *potager* at Villandry. Pastel masses of cactus planted on terraces catch the light from the rising sun and are intended to be viewed from above. A rushing stream, reminiscent of Japanese gardens, races down a chute carefully lined with irregularly shaped stones.

In Michigan a similarly dramatic set of postmodern gardens are located between the Kellogg World Headquarters and the river, in the Battle Creek Linear Park. Here, a bold terraced lawn is punctuated with undulating linear concrete retaining walls, which accent the bubblers in the large reflective pool. Rocks placed in native grasses soften a strong straight line leading

to the corporate headquarters. A geometrical pool of water, viewed from a vine-covered pergola, fits neatly into a checkerboard of lawn and concrete. In an adjacent garden, spring flowering trees and comfortable wooden benches line a meandering walk. These gardens connect along the river to the equally beautiful gardens near the W. K. Kellogg Foundation. The yearning for a natural environment, along with the desire to clean up old industrial sites, has been the motivation for these gardens, which

Kellogg World Headquarters.
ABOVE: Undulating retaining walls in lawn. Photo by Balthazar Korab. **BELOW: Grid pattern with pergola and pool with bubblers.**

LEFT: Historic Kellogg home near naturalized stream in Battle Creek Linear Park.

ABOVE: Underground railroad sculpture, Battle Creek.

ABOVE RIGHT: Restored edge, Battle Creek Linear Park.

BELOW AND BELOW RIGHT: Leonardo da Vinci's Horse: The American Horse, Frederik Meijer Gardens, Grand Rapids, Michigan. Photo below right by Balthazar Korab.

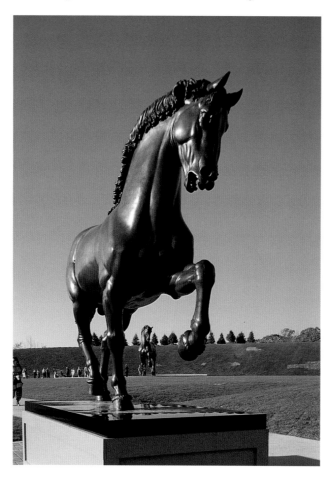

include the relocation of the historic Kellogg home and its formal garden. A bronze sculpture commemorating the Underground Railroad stands near perennial gardens cared for by the Leila Arboretum. The restoration of the river's edge into a scenic series of rapids, ledges, and native plants, shows the reestablishment and embellishment of the natural landscape. The Kellogg gardens represent a wonderful integration of both urban and garden design.

Some of the newest postmodern gardens in the state are the Botanical Gardens and Sculpture Park at the Frederik Meijer Gardens in Grand Rapids. These gardens were planned around six major themes: perennial gardens, greenhouse gardens, nature trails, sculptural gardens, historic gardens, and the "New American Garden." The most dramatic feature in these gardens is the twenty-four-foot-high, fifteen-ton, bronze horse known as Leonardo da Vinci's Horse: American Horse. This creation which was inspired by Leonardo da Vinci's drawings, was cast in Beacon, New York as only one of two, with help from Frederik Meijer. Now placed as a centerpiece in the sculptural gardens, the American Horse has made these gardens internationally known. The

Leslie E. Tassell English Perennial & Bulb Garden contains a collection of herbaceous flowers that provide interest and color throughout the year and are reminiscent of English cottage gardens. The Lena Meijer Conservatory is the largest greenhouse in Michigan and is designed in the international style. The gardens inside provide warmth and diversity. A Victorian-Era tea garden with ferns, citrus, elegant marble columns, and a lovely fountain create a wonderful setting for a cup of tea in the winter. The tropical gardens reach to the sky and allow the visitor to walk over and around a flowing stream. A waterfall leaps down a rock wall and splashes into a pool surrounded by bold foliage, while bronze sculptures of animals play in the water. Outside the greenhouse, a nature trail

Lena Meijer Conservatory, Frederik Meijer Gardens, Grand Rapids, Michigan.
Photo by Balthazar Korab.

Frederik Meijer Gardens, Grand Rapids, Michigan. TOP: **Tropical foliage.**
ABOVE: **Monument to Gwen Frostic in the Woodland Shade Garden.**
ABOVE RIGHT: **Sculpture at entry to garden.**
RIGHT: **A sweep of native plants and grasses in the New American Garden.**
Photo by Balthazar Korab.

allows the visitor to walk over a wetland area and through a woodland garden, which is named for the well-loved Michigan artist and poet, Gwen Frostic. The entry to the botanical garden and sculpture park is surround by large sculptures and a broad sweep of vegetation planted in a style known as the "New American Garden." The shape of this garden is defined with masses of daffodils and asters blooming in their seasons. Dried foliage and seed pods are allowed to stay on the perennial material through the winter, adding a picturesque texture in the snow. This way of handling native and naturalized plant materials allows for a low-maintenance garden full of diverse colors and textures.

The campus at Michigan State University continues its tradition as a leader in garden design with the recent creation of a large horticultural garden adjacent to the new Plant Science Building. The gardens are designed in distinct groupings that combine a wide range of styles and ideas, including a resemblance of the heart of the old park-like north campus with its relaxed lines, a natural pond, and replicas of the historic lampposts and lanterns. The annual, or display garden, reflects a formal theme with its simplified version of classical architecture in garden structures. An axis leads visitors to the white latticework of the formal rose gardens to the south.

The rose gardens are planted in two different four-parts patterns with a path punctuated by white carpentry work, hidden away from the perennial gardens by deep evergreen plantings. The perennial gardens are attached to the formal garden by a large circular compass, which rotates the visitors from one style of garden to the next. The perennial gardens, with many curvilinear flowerbeds cut into the lawn and planted with a wonderful combination of perennials, provide color from March until late October. A large curricular pergola with classical columns and a tree of life planted in the center graces the entry to the perennial gardens. In the parking lot, a fourteen-foot peacock with a thirty-five-foot spreading tail, planted in annuals each year, greets guests and serves as a reminder of the fun the Victorians had with gardens.

Wedged between these garden and railroad tracks is the Children's Garden,

ABOVE: Historic Lamppost in the heart of park-like North Campus, Michigan State University, East Lansing.

LEFT: Curvilinear flowerbed cut into the lawn, Horticulture Demonstration Gardens, Michigan State University, East Lansing.

built to nurture young imaginations. Examples of the educational quality of the garden include the cereal garden, featuring grains for making breakfast cereals; the pizza garden, full of plants that go into making a pizza planted in a concrete "crust"; and, a butterfly garden shaped like a butterfly. The rainbow garden is an arc painted in bright colors, lined on each side with vegetables and plants favored by African Americans, Asian Americans, Mexican American, and Native Americans, as well as a "pioneer"

garden. An Alice-in-Wonderland maze made of cedar hedges leads to a secret garden inspired by Frances Hodgson Burnett's novel. A charming Monet bridge arches over a water garden featuring an unusual jumping-jet fountain. The garden has been built on a very small scale, delighting children and their parents. This garden has won numerous awards and has encouraged other public gardens in Michigan to create their own versions. Applewood, Fernwood, Leila, and the Dow Gardens now have special areas built for children.

Many public gardens are in the process of being enlarged and improved. The Fernwood Nature Center and the Botanic Garden and Arts and Crafts Center, in Niles, is a museum of living plants and natural ecosystems. A master plan for the 105-acre center guides the development of a series of formal and informal gardens. A prairie reconstruction, which has matured over thirty years, allows visitors to wander through a mowed path similar to a labyrinth. A dovecote and herb garden replicate similar gardens from colonial times. Another master plan was completed in January of 2000 for the Leila Arboretum Society in Battle Creek. When these gardens are complete they will include a children's adventure garden, a water garden, and expanded display

Children's Garden, Michigan State University. OPPOSITE: Rainbow Garden with vegetable gardens from various cultures. Photo by Balthazar Korab. **TOP: Pizza garden. ABOVE: Bubble fountain and Monet Bridge.**

Pavilion in conifer collection, Hidden Lake Garden, Tipton.

gardens. Hidden Lakes Garden, part of the MSU complex, has recently incorporated into its design a miniature conifer collection complete with a Japanese-style pavilion overlooking the garden.

Michigan has looked to Europe numerous times in the past for gardening ideas and will most likely continue to do so. The enormous abandoned industrials sites along the Detroit River are similar to those in the Ruhr Valley of Germany. The Emcher Park Program for the environmental improvement of the Ruhr Valley, a government-led effort to reclaim a fifty-mile stretch, includes the Duisburg Nord Landscape Park. This urban garden is a revolution in conceptualization of garden potential, as a huge steelworks has been transformed into an ecological park. The Duisberg Park is based on an appreciation of steelworks, which have been conserved in a way that makes them safe enough to climb, but allows them to rust. It is a gigantic playground and provides views all over the valley. There are two fundamental ecological principles guiding the development. The first is to recycle building materials; for example, bricks are ground up to make the aggregate for red concrete, and steel parts are welded together to make park furniture. The second idea allows polluted water to be cleaned through an observable natural process. A walkway has been reconstructed from a former overhead railway, allowing visitors to walk across the bunkers and look down into the gardens and basins filled with water lilies. Some vegetation has been planted in a formal pattern and other vegetation has been allowed to regenerate naturally, trapping and filtering pollutants from the water. A hint of this concept is seen in the Upper Peninsula in Iron county, where a trail through the old mining sites has been planted with apple trees and wildflowers, while mining relics are used as sculptures.

Duisberg Nord Landscape Park, Germany.

Public gardens have been built in Michigan since gardener Pierre d'Argenteuil arrived with Detroit's first French settlers in 1701. Michigan citizens founded the first Agricultural Society in the Midwest. Michigan Agricultural College was the first public institution to teach landscape gardening as a required course, and created its own set of public grounds. Many citizens who accumulated great wealth in the early twentieth century gave their elaborate estates to the public as pleasure grounds, and most universities and colleges have landscaped campuses that are sources of great pride. Michigan cities have beautified their rivers with linear parks, and filled their streets with flowers. Public gardens in Michigan feature fountains as grand as any in Europe. The unique bronze American Horse in Grand Rapids, the antique Roman columns at Cranbrook, the leading-edge garden design in Battle Creek, and the nationally acclaimed Children's Garden at Michigan State University make Michigan gardens unique. But the fact that Michigan has more gardens open to the public than almost any other state in the union makes Michigan a premier garden state.

Michigan's Public Gardens

Northern Michigan Area

Mackinac Island
• Grand Hotel Gardens

Marquette
• Marquette Prison

Mid-Michigan Area

East Lansing
• Michigan State University - North Campus
• Michigan State University - South Campus

Flint
• Applewood, Charles Stewart Mott Estate

Lansing
• Capitol Grounds
• Cooley Park
• Francis Park

Midland
• Dow Gardens

Saginaw
• Tokushima Saginaw Friendship Center

West Michigan Area

Battle Creek
• Kellogg World Headquarters
• Riverfront

Grand Rapids
• Frederik Meijer Gardens

Holland
• Streetscape

Marshall
• Downtown

Niles
• Fernwood Botanical Garden and Nature Center

Ann Arbor—Jackson Area

Ann Arbor
• Matthaei Botanical Gardens, University of Michigan
• Nichols Arboretum, University of Michigan

Hillsdale
• Slayton Arboretum, Hillsdale College

Jackson
• Sparks Park and Cascade Fountain

Somerset Center
• McCourtie Park

Tipton
• Hidden Lake Garden, Michigan State University

Detroit Area

Bloomfield Hills
• Cranbrook Educational Community (3)

Dearborn
• Fair Lane, Henry Ford Estate (4)
• Greenfield Village, Clara B. Ford Gardens (5)

Detroit
• Belle Isle Park, Anna Scripps Whitcomb Conservatory (2)
• Elmwood Cemetery (6)
• Fisher Mansion and Bhaktivedanta Cultural Center (7)
• Wayne State University Campus (8)

Grosse Pointe
• Alger House and Veteran's War Memorial (9)

Grosse Pointe Shores
• Edsel and Eleanor Ford House and Gardens (10)

Rochester
• Oakland University, Meadowbrook Hall (1)

Royal Oak
• Hills Detroit Zoological Park (11)

Warren
• General Motors Technical Center (12)

Michigan's Public Gardens

	Former Private Estate	Arboretum/Botanical	Children's Garden/Activities	Conservatory	Formal European Elements	Fountains	Garden Pavilions	Gift Shop	Herb Garden	Registration as Historic Site	House Tour/Museum/Gallery	Japanese Garden Elements	English Landscape Style	Nature Trails	Perennial Beds	River/Lake/Stream	Annual Beds	Rose Garden	Sculptures	Modern Style	Postmodern Style	Arts and Crafts Style
Alger House, Grosse Pointe War Memorial	•				•	•				•	•				•	•	•	•	•			
Applewood, Charles S. Mott Estate	•		•		•	•		•	•	•			•		•		•	•	•			•
Cooley, Scott, and Francis Parks	•			•	•					•					•	•	•					•
Cranbrook House	•				•	•			•	•	•	•	•		•		•	•	•			•
Edsel and Eleanor Ford House and Gardens	•		•		•	•	•		•	•	•		•		•		•	•				•
Fair Lane, Henry Ford Estate	•		•		•	•	•	•	•	•	•		•		•	•	•	•				•
Fisher Mansion and Bhaktivedanta Cultural Center	•				•	•				•	•				•			•				
Hidden Lake Garden	•	•		•	•	•	•					•	•	•	•		•					
Kellogg Conference Center Gardens	•	•			•					•			•		•		•					•
Meadow Brook Hall	•		•			•	•			•	•				•		•					
Dow Gardens	•	•	•	•			•	•	•			•							•	•		•
Belle Isle Park and Whitcomb Conservatory		•	•	•						•		•			•		•		•			•
Centennial Park and Holland Streetscape					•	•				•					•		•		•			
Cranbrook Art Museum					•	•			•	•	•				•		•	•	•	•		
Detroit Zoological Park		•	•	•	•			•	•				•		•		•	•	•	•		•
Elmwood Cemetary		•				•				•			•									
Fernwood Botanic Garden and Nature Preserve		•	•		•	•	•							•	•							•
Frederik Meijer Gardens		•	•	•	•	•	•	•					•		•		•	•	•	•	•	
General Motors Technical Center					•											•				•		
Grand Hotel Gardens						•							•		•		•					•
Greenfield Village			•		•		•		•	•	•				•	•	•		•			•
Kellogg Gardens, Battle Creek Riverfront						•									•	•	•		•		•	
Leila Arboretum and Botanical Garden		•	•	•	•	•	•						•		•	•	•					
Marquette Prison					•	•				•						•						•
Matthaei Botanical Gardens		•		•	•		•	•					•	•	•	•	•			•		•
McCourtie Park			•			•	•						•			•						•
Michigan State Capitol Square		•			•	•				•	•				•		•					
MSU Horticulture Gardens		•	•	•	•	•	•	•							•		•	•	•	•	•	
MSU Lewis Arboretum		•			•							•	•		•		•					
MSU North Campus		•			•										•	•	•					•
Nichols Arboretum		•					•			•			•	•	•	•						
Slayton Arboretum		•	•		•		•		•				•		•	•	•					•
Sparks Park and Cascade Fountain					•	•							•		•	•						
Tokushima Friendship Center												•			•				•			•
Veldheer Demonstration Gardens					•			•							•		•			•	•	
Wayne State University Campus				•	•															•	•	
Windmill Island			•			•										•						

Garden Elements and Terms

Allée: French term for alley. This is a narrow passageway between walls, high fences or tall, closely set vegetation such as arborvitae or trees, which are pruned high or pleached. The allée focuses the eye to a particular point where a fountain or sculpture is often positioned.

Amphitheater: An outdoor elliptical or circular space surrounded by rising tiers or seats. It was first made popular by the Greeks as settings for their dramas. Often they include a stage with a backdrop or a dense hedge.

Annual beds: Planting areas for flowers whose life cycle is one season. They must be replanted each year. Many of the most colorful garden flowers are annuals.

Arbor: Other terms for the same feature are pergola, bower, gazebo, and pavilion. It is an open freestanding structure that supplies shade in a garden. It usually has a lattice framework with columns, which will support vines and roses.

Arboretum: A plot of land where trees or shrubs are grown for scientific or educational study, either individually or in groupings. The plants are often labeled.

Art Nouveau: A French term for "new art." A decorative art movement in European architecture beginning in the 1880s and reaching its peak in the United States about 1910. It is characterized by flowing and sinuous naturalistic ornaments and the avoidance of traditional architectural patterns.

Arts and Crafts movement: A philosophy that embraces the use of regional natural materials and effects and looks back to the fine workmanship of goods produced under the medieval guild system-1990s to 1918.

Asymmetry: The opposite of bilateral symmetry. This term applies to anything that has no point, line, or plan about which parts are arranged in a regular or geometrical fashion.

Axis: The lines that divide formal gardens into numerous parts and sections. There can be one or many axes and cross-axes.

Baroque: A style of art and architecture characterized by extensive or extravagant ornamentation, curved rather than straight lines, and classical forms. It flourished in France in the 1700s.

Bauhaus: The common name of a design school founded in Dessau, Germany in 1918. The principle of the school was "form follows function." The ideals of the school led to the International Style of architecture.

Beaux arts: A French term for the fine arts. It is associated with design that is formal, axial and refers back to the classical style of architecture. The École Des Beaux Arts in Paris was the center of the design style.

Berceau: A network of arbored pathways in a pattern similar to a parterre with small fountains and seating under the arbor.

Biennial: A plant whose life cycle is of two seasons. They are usually at their best only for the second season.

Bilateral: Two matching sides arranged on opposite sides of an axis, such as butterfly wings. It is often used with the term symmetry.

Bollard: Any short vertical post of stone, metal, or wood placed in the landscape and used to control vehicular circulation while allowing free movement by pedestrians. The posts are often decorative and include lighting.

Bridge: Structure that allow paths to cross over water. Often used for decorative purposes, to focus a visitor on a view or for seating.

Broderie parterre: A French expression for embroidery on the ground. The decorative arrangement of ornamental flowers mixed with gravels of different colors on the ground to be viewed from above. Also called *parterre de broderie* and similar to knot gardens

Carpet bedding: A popular Victorian Era style of arranging colorful and showy annuals in geometric patterns within a grass lawn. Schemes are changed each year.

Cascade: A natural or human-made waterfall or a series of small waterfalls. Often the basins are shaped into chains or shells.

Chateau: A French word for a castle or a fine country estate, including the residence and the grounds.

Children's garden: A garden designed specifically for young children with small-scale elements, colorful flowers, and hands on opportunities for play.

Classical: In accordance with the Greek and Roman Classic orders in arts, literature and architecture.

Cloister: A rectangular courtyard surrounded by an open arcade. Often associated with medieval monasteries.

Conservatory: A glass building used like a greenhouse for growing tropical and dessert plants. The conservatory is usually a very attractive building harping back to the Victorian Era.

Cottage garden: A small residential garden, utilitarian and ornamental, popular in England and Holland. They were generally asymmetrical, but made use of formal features such as clipped hedges, bedding plants, flowers for cutting, turf, gravel paths, sundials, small fountains and trellises. Associated with the Arts and Crafts movement.

Country place era: A period in American history marked by the creation of many large residential properties in the countryside. 1880s to 1930s

Deciduous: A term referring to trees and shrubs that shed their leaves each autumn or at the end of their active growing season.

Demonstration gardens: Gardens created for exhibition of plant materials and design forms to give ideas to visitors.

Dovecote: A small house or box with chambers for nesting pigeons or doves, usually above the ground, on the grounds or an English estate.

Eclecticism: The practice of selecting from various styles of architecture, usually in order to form a new system or style of design. Combining historical styles of various cultures.

English Landscape school of design: A style of landscape gardening which developed in England in the middle of the eighteenth century. It was opposed to anything that was formal in the landscape. It requires a large landscape where the lawn could sweep unobstructed to the house. Scenes are created which were bucolic and pastoral.

Espalier: A tree, shrub or vine trained to grow flat against a wall or on a trellis.

Exotic: Of a foreign origin or character. When the term is applied to plants it means it is not native to the area.

Formal layout: Garden design plan in a very regular pattern with axis, geometry, sight lines, and bilateral symmetry.

Fountain: An artificial jet of or jets of water, which spill into a basin or basins, which are often decorated with carvings and sculptures. There is a tremendous variety is size and form.

Functionalism: A theory that emphasizes the need to design or adapt structures to their ultimate function for they way in which they are to be used. The idea relates to the Bauhaus movement.

Gardenesque: A garden style popular in the Victorian era identified with exotic plant material and many garden elements from foreign places. Highly ornamented.

Gazebo: Other terms for the same feature are pergola, bower, arbor, and pavilion. An open, freestanding structure that supplies shade in a garden. It usually had a lattice framework with columns, which will support vines and roses.

Grotto: An Italian word for a natural or artificial cave built as a shady moist retreat from the heat.

Ground cover: A low growing evergreen plant with small leaves typically less than twelve inches tall. They are planted close together to form a carpet like effect.

Herb garden: A garden developed for the cultivation of herbs and often laid out formally and ornamental in appearance.

Historic preservation: A broad term meaning to save or protect from destruction structures that have historic value for our society.

Historic restoration: The process of accurately recovering the form and details of a property and its setting as it appeared at a particular period of time.

Japanese garden: Gardens which take their form and elements from Japan. Typically they are small, borrow views, minituralize natural elements, include water or raked sand or gravel, and are used for contemplation.

Knot gardens: An early English expression of a garden composed of small hedges, bedding plants and other ground covers planted in elaborate designs and patterns lying close to the ground. They are meant to be viewed from above. Similar to *parterre de broderie*.

Labyrinth: A network of interconnecting passages either carved in the stone floor of a medieval church or formed of clipped evergreen hedges, a maze.

Maze: A network of interconnecting passages either carved in the stone floor of a medieval church or formed of clipped evergreen hedges, a labyrinth.

Naturalistic landscape: The quality of being like nature rather than human-made. Characteristic of the style are curvilinear lines, rolling topography with clumps of trees and a winding stream or pond.

Neoclassical: Literally, "new Classicism, " characterized by a more academic use of classical features.

Palladian: Relating to a typical classical Roman style of architecture popularized by Andrea Palladio, and Italian architect, 1518-1580. It is similar to neoclassical, but came at an earlier day and is related to the English Landscape school.

Parterre de Broderie: A French expression for embroidery on the ground. The decorative arrangement of ornamental flowers mixed with gravels of different colors on the ground to be viewed from above. Also called *broderie parterre* and similar to knot gardens.

Pavilion: Other terms for the same feature are pergola, bower, gazebo, and arbor. An open freestanding structure which supplies shade in a garden. It usually had a lattice framework with columns, which will support vines and roses.

Pergola: Other terms for the same feature are arbor, bower, gazebo, and pavilion. An open freestanding structure which supplies shade in a garden. It usually had a lattice framework with columns, which will support vines and roses.

Picturesque: The term to describe one of the attitudes of taste toward landscape gardening between 1785 and 1835. The idea is that the same kind of beauty that is agreeable in a picture can be created in the landscape. Jane Austen novels take place in this type of landscape.

Pleached: Pruning in a fashion to interlace the tops of trees or other plants to form a tunnel-like archway over a walkway.

Potager: The French word for vegetable garden. The French usually mix flowers with vegetables and plant them in a formal ornamental pattern.

Promenade: A walk for strolling, especially in a public place. Generally laid out with a view and lined with trees.

Rock garden: A garden whose surface is primarily rocks, sometimes very large, with many herbs and small plants integrated with the stones.

Rose garden: A small formal garden generally placed away from the main garden and surrounded by a hedge. The purpose is to display roses, which look their best for a short season and therefore should not be part of the main garden.

Sculpture: Artwork made of a variety of materials, free standing, and placed in the landscape to be focused on and appreciated.

Sight line: The line along which a person in a space can look down and view a series of spaces. In baroque design the line often focus on the setting sun.

Symmetrical: Two matching sides arranged on opposite sides of an axis. It is often used with the term bilateral

Tapis Vert: A French tem for a square of rectangular manicured grass area, often used to open a view to an important garden element.

Topiary: Pruned evergreen plants trained into geometrical or sculptural forms.

Trellis: An open framework or lattice used as a support for growing vines or other plants. Often they cover a walkway.

Victorian era: The time period in which Queen Victoria was on the British throne. It is associated with gardening as a fine art and with amateurs enthusiastically participating in plant nurturing and landscape gardening-1837-1901

Vista: A confined segment of a view usually toward a terminal or dominant element or feature.

Bibliography

Adams, Steven. *The Arts and Crafts Movement.* Secaucus, N.J.: Chartwell Books, 1987.

Agar, Madeline. *Garden Design in Theory and Practice.* Philadelphia: J. B. Lippincott Company, 1911. This book concentrates on garden design with stress laid upon content and form. The author purposely omitted everything of a purely horticultural nature.

Bailey, Liberty Hyde. *The Gardener.* 1900. Reprint, New York: Macmillan Company, 1925. "I want the reader clearly to understand what I intend in this book. It considers only the growing and care of plants. The landscape the layout of grounds and the adornment of premises, the appreciation of beauty and interest in plants are considered in the Manual of Gardening, but not directly here" (vi).

———. *The Rural Science Series, Garden Making.* 1898. Reprint, New York: Macmillan Company, 1909.

Balmori, Diana, Diane Kostial McGuire, and Eleanor M. McPeck. *Beatrix Farrand's American Landscapes: Her Gardens and Campuses.* Millwood, N.Y.: Sagapress, 1985.

Beal, W. J. *History of the Michigan Agricultural College and Biographical Sketches of Trustees and Professor.* East Lansing, Mich.: Agricultural College, 1915. Beal's personal recollections of the campus development where he became a faculty member in 1871 and developed the first botanical gardens west of the Allegheny mountains.

Berg, Herbert Andrew. *Bela Hubbard 1841—1896. A Biographical Sketch.* East Lansing: n.p., 1967. A typewritten paper that includes *Memorial for a State Agricultural College in Michigan.*

Berrall, Julia S., *The Garden, An Illustrated History.* New York: The Viking Press, 1966.

Beveridge, Charles E., and Paul Rocheleau. *Frederick Law Olmsted, Designing the American Landscape.* New York: Rizzoli, 1995.

Birnbaum, Charles, and Robin Karson. *Pioneers of American Landscape.* New York: McGraw-Hill, 2000.

Buczacki, Stefan. *Creating a Victorian Flower Garden.* New York: Weidenfeld & Nicholson, 1988.

Buildings of Detroit. Detroit, Mich.: Wayne State University Press, 1968. Contains photographs of early French gardens, although this book deal primarily with buildings.

Church, Thomas D. *Gardens are for People,* 3d ed. Ed. Grace Hall, and Michael Laurie. N.p.: University of California Press, 1995.

Damrosch, Barbara. *Theme Gardens.* Illus. Karl W. Stuecklen. New York: Workman Publishers, 1982.

De Charlevoix, Pierre. *Journal of a Voyage to North-America.* Ann Arbor, Mich.: University Microfilms, Inc., 1996.

De Long, David G.. *Frank Lloyd Wright Designs for an American Landscape, 1922—1932.* New York: Harry N. Abrams, Inc., 1996.

Dorf, Philip. *Liberty Hyde Bailey, An Informal Biography.* Ithaca, N.Y.: Cornell University Press, 1956.

Douglas, William Lake, et al. *Garden Design: History, Principles, Elements Practice.* Intro. John Brookes. Photo. Derek Fell. New York: Simon and Schuster, 1984.

Downing, Andrew Jackson. *A Treatise on the Theory and Practice of Landscape Gardening, Adapted to North America.* New York: Wiley and Putnam, 1841. The author hoped to contribute to the improvement of country residences; thus, the topics listed in a lengthy subtitle included Horticultural Notices and General Principles of the Art, Directions for laying out Grounds and arranging Plantations, the Description and Cultivation of Hardy Trees, Decorative Accompaniments to the House and Grounds, the Formation of Pieces of Artificial Water, Flower Gardens and With Remarks on Rural Architecture. It quickly became the best selling and most widely influential book of its type published in 19th century American (Schuyler, *Apostle of Taste*, 28).

———. "Public Cemeteries and Gardens." In *Rural Essays.* Ed. George William Curtis. New York: Da Capo Press, 1974.

Duchscherer, Paul, and Douglas Keister. *Outside the Bungalow: America's Arts and Crafts Garden.* New York: Penguin Studio, 1999.

Eaton, Leonard K. *Landscape Artist in America, The Life and Work of Jens Jensen.* Chicago: University of Chicago Press, 1964.

Eckert, Kathryn Bishop. *Buildings of Michigan.* New York: Oxford University Press, 1993; Lanham, Md.: Altamira Press, 1997.

Enge, Torsten Olaf, and Carl Friedrich Schroer. *Garden Architecture in Europe, 1450-1800, From the Villa Garden of the Italian Renaissance to the English Landscape Garden.* Cologne, Germany: Taschen, 1992.

Farmer, Silas. *History of Detroit and Wayne County and Early Michigan, A Chronological Cyclopedia of the Past and Present.* 1890. Reprint, Detroit, Mich.: Gale Research 1969.

Favretti, Rudy J. *Gardens and Landscapes of Virginia.* Photo. Richard Cheek. Little Compton, R.I.: Fort Church Publishers, 1993.

Favretti, Rudy J., and Gordon P. DeWolf. *Colonial Gardens.* Barre, Mass.: Barre Publishers, 1972.

Favretti, Rudy J., and Joy Putman Favretti. *Landscapes and Gardens for Historic Buildings.* 2d ed. American Association for State and Local History Book Series. Nashville: Tennessee, 1991.

———. *For Every House a Garden: A Guide for Reproducing Period Gardens.* Hanover, N.H.: University Press of New England, 1990.

Ferry, W. Hawkins. *The Buildings of Detroit.* Rev. ed. Detroit, Mich: Wayne State University Press, 1980.

Festing, Sally. *Gertrude Jekyll.* London: Viking, 1991.

Fitzgerald, Robert. *Art Nouveau, Architecture and Design Library.* New York: Friedman/Fairfax Publishers, Michael Friedman Publishing Group, Inc., 1997.

French, Jere Stuart. *The California Garden and the Landscape Architects Who Shaped It.* N.p.: The Landscape Architecture Foundation, 1993.

Gothein, Marie Luise. *A History of Garden Art.* Ed. Walter P. Wright. Trans. Mrs. Archer-Hind. 2 vols. London: J. M. Dent and Sons Limited; New York: E. P. Dutton and Co., Ltd., 1928.

Grese, Robert E., *Jens Jensen Maker of Natural Parks and Gardens.* Baltimore, Md.: John Hopkins University Press, 1992.

Hamlin, Stephen F. *Book of Garden Plans, Twenty Blueprint Plans and Many Half-Tone Illustrations.* New York: Doubleday, Page, and Company, 1916.

Hanna, Jennifer Grace. *Ornamental Garden Design: The Rise of Floricultural Publications and the Role of James Vick, Rochester Seed House Owner.* Master's Thesis, Cornell University, 1997.

Hedrick, U. P. *A History of Horticulture in America to 1860.* New York: Oxford University Press, 1950. "French gardens were established in Michigan and Canada in 1701 and it was a gardening center for 150 years" (302).

———. *The Land of the Crooked Tree.* Detroit, Mich.: Wayne State University Press, 1986. The Land of the Crooked Tree is on the northern tip of the lower peninsula of Michigan and was one of the last forest regions in eastern America to be settled by whites.

Holden, Robert, and Hudson, Jennifer. *International Landscape Design*. London: Laurence King Publishing, 1996. Discusses postindustrial parks and recreation, ecology, conservation offices and institutions, urban design, and housing in major European and American cities.

Hubbard, Bela. *Memorials of a Half-Century in Michigan and the Lake Region*. New York: B. P. Putnam's Sons, The Knickerbocker Press, 1888.

———. *Memorials of a Half-Century in Michigan and the Lake Region*. 1887. Reprint, New York: G. P. Putnam's Sons, 1888.

Hunt, John Dixon. *The Figure in the Landscape: Poetry, Painting, and Gardening during the Eighteenth Century*. Baltimore, Md.: John Hopkins University Press, 1976

Jekyll, Gertrude. *Colour Schemes for the Flower Gardens*. Intro. Richard Bisgrove. 1919. Reprint, London: Charles Scribner's Sons, 1988.

Jekyll, Gertrude, and Lawrence Weaver. *Gardens for Small Country Houses*. New York: Charles Scribner's Sons, 1913. Reprint, England: Antique Collection Club, 1981.

Jellicoe, Geoffrey, and Susan Jellicoe. *The Landscape of Man, Shaping the Environment from Prehistory to the Present Day*. 3d ed. New York, N.Y.: Thames and Hudson, 1995.

Jellicoe, Geoffrey, et al., eds. *The Oxford Companion to Gardens*. Oxford University Press, 1986.

Kemp, Edward. *How to Lay Out a Garden, Intended as a General Guide in Choosing, Forming, or Improving an Estate, with Reference to Both Design and Execution*. London: Bradbury and Evans, 1864. One of the original textbooks for the Landscape Gardening classes taught at MAC by Prentiss in 1863 and by Prentiss at Cornell in 1868.

King, Louisa Yeomans, "Mrs. Francis King." *The Flower Garden Day by Day*. Intro. Gertrude Jekyll. New York: Frederick A. Stokes Company, 1927.

———. *The Well-Considered Garden*. New York: Scribner, 1915.

Kuhn, Madison. Michigan State: *The First Hundred Years, 1855-1955*. East Lansing: Michigan State University Press, 1955.

Laurie, Michael, *The Introduction to Landscape Architecture*, second edition. Englewood Cliffs, N.J., Prentice Hall, 1986.

Lautner, Harold W. From an Oak Opening, A Record of the Development of the Campus Park of Michigan State University, 1855—1969. 2 vols. Michigan State University Archives, 1977.

Mann, *Landscape Architecture, An Illustrated History in Timelines, Site Plans, and Biography*. John Wiley and Sons, Inc., 1993.

McAlester, Virginia, and Lee McAlester. A *Field Guide to American Houses*. Drawings by Lauren Jarrett and model house drawings by Juan Rodriguez-Arnaiz. 1894. Reprint, New York: Knopf, 1996.

Mosser, Monique, and Georges Teyssot. *The History of Garden Design: The Western Tradition from the Renaissance to the Present Day*. New York: Thames and Hudson, 1991.

Newton, Norman T. *Design on the Land, The Development of Landscape Architecture*. Boston, Mass.: Belknap Press of Harvard University Press, 1971.

Noble, Allen, G. *To Build in a New Land, Ethnic Landscapes in North America*. Baltimore, Md.: Johns Hopkins University Press, 1992.

Ogrin, Dusan. *The World Heritage of Gardens*. New York: Thames and Hudson, 1993.

Otis, Charles Herbert. *Michigan Trees, A Handbook of the Native and Most Important Introduced Species*. 1915. Reprint, Ann Arbor: University of Michigan Botanical Garden and Arboretum, 1926.

Packard, Robert. *Encyclopedia of American Architecture*. 2d ed. New York: McGraw-Hill Inc., 1995.

Pfeiffer, Bruce Brooks. *Frank Lloyd Wright Master Builder*. New York: Rizzoli, 1993.

Pregill, Philip and Nancy Volkman. *Landscapes in History, Design and Planning in the Western Tradition*. New York: Van Nostrand Reinhold, 1993.

Roberts, Edith A., and Elsa Rehmann. *American Plants for American Gardens, Plant Ecology—The Study of Plants in Relation to Their Environment*. New York: Macmillan Company, 1929.

Rodgers, Andrew Denny, III. *Liberty Hyde Bailey, A Story of American Plant Science*. Princeton, N.J.: Princeton University Press, 1949.

Saudan-Skira, Sylvia, and Michel Saudan. *Orangeries, Palaces of Glass—Their History and Development*. Köln, Germany: Evergreen, 1998.

Schmitt, Peter J. *Back to Nature, The Arcadian Myth in Urban America*. New York: Oxford University Press, 1969.

Schuyler, David. *Apostle of Taste: Andrew Jackson Downing 1815—1852*. Baltimore, Md.: Johns Hopkins University Press, 1996.

Sedgwick, Mabel Cabot. *The Garden Month by Month*. New York: F. A. Stokes Company, 1907.

Semback, Klaus-Jurgen. *Art Nouveau Utopia: Reconciling the Irreconcilable*. Trans. Charity Scott. Köln, Germany: Taschen, 1999.

Sloane, David Charles. *The Last Great Necessity; Cemeteries in American History*. Baltimore, Md.: John Hopkins University Press, 1991. An overview of cemetery movements in America. It discusses the diversity of burial customs and places and divides the subject into four time periods.

Sommer, Robin Langley, ed. *The Arts and Crafts Movement*. Secaucus, N.J.: Chartwell Books, Inc, 1995.

Steele, Fletcher. *Design in the Little Garden*. Little Garden Series. New York: Atlantic Monthly Press, 1924.

Stoller, Ezra, and General Motors Public Relations Staff. "Where Today Meets Tomorrow, General Motors Technical Center, and Explanation of the New Technical Center with Architectural Plans, and Photographs, 1950s." N.p., N.d.

Stuart, David. *The Garden Triumphant: A Victorian Legacy*. New York: Harper and Row, 1988.

Thacker, Christopher, *The History of Gardens*. University of California Press, 1979.

Tishler, William H. *Midwestern Landscape Architecture*. Urbana and Chicago: University of Illinois Press, 2000. Profiles the innovators in landscape architecture who, around the turn of the twentieth century, ventured into the nation's heartland to develop a new style of design that celebrated the native Midwestern landscape.

——, ed. *American Landscape Architecture: Designers and Places*. Washington D.C.: National Trust for Historic Preservation, Preservation Press, 1989. Reprint, New York: Wiley, 1996

Van Rensselaer, Mrs. Schuyler. *Art Out-of-Doors; Hints on Good Taste in Gardening*. 1903. Reprint, New York: Charles Scribner's Sons, 1959.

Verey, Rosemary, and Ellen Samuels. *The American Woman's Garden*. Boston: Little, Brown and Company, 1984.

Waugh, F. A. *Landscape Gardening: How to Lay Out a Garden, by Edward Kemp, Landscape Gardener*. Rev. ed. New York: John Wiley and Sons, 1911.

Wharton, Edith. *Italian Villas and Their Gardens*. Illus. Maxfield Parrish. New York: The Century Co., 1904.

Wilder, Louise Beebe. *Colour In My Garden*. New York: Doubleday, Page and Company, 1927.

OPPOSITE: The campus of Michigan State University.

Acknowledgments

Children's Garden, Michigan State University. Photo by Balthazar Korab.

I have been fortunate in the past thirty years in having the opportunity to listen to many distinguished landscape architecture and garden historians; to travel to gardens throughout the United States and Europe; and to teach landscape architecture history to thousands of students at Michigan State University and the University of Arizona.

Several people have been indispensable in the development of this story. My husband, Earl W. Rutz, believed in this book so strongly that he traveled to every garden (many several times) taking photographs. My oldest daughter, Kristi Rutz-Robbins, dissected the text and made it sing. My teacher and advisor at the University of California, Berkeley, Michael Laurie, to whom I will always be a student and my dear friend and colleague at Michigan State University, June Thomas, both inspired me to keep writing.

In addition, this book would not have been possible without the help of many colleagues at Michigan State University. Provost Lou Anna Simon supported the concept of a book on Michigan gardens. Help within the programs of Landscape Architecture and Urban and Regional Planning came from Tom Cocozzoli, our librarian; Dawn Brown, Bets Caldwell, and Pat Daughenbaugh, our secretaries; computer experts, Michael Lipsey and Wilson Ndovie; faculty members past and present, particularly Michael Hodges, who left me his slides of English gardens when he passed away in 1991; and not least, the students over the years who have challenged and informed me. Julie Loehr, Fred Bohm and Elizabeth Demers at Michigan State University Press, and graphic artist Tom Kachadurian, all believed in the book. Their efforts turned vision into reality.

My very dear friend Merle Heidemann read early editions of the text. Balthazar Korab allowed us to use some of his most spectacular photographs of Michigan gardens. The members of the Garden Clubs of Michigan for twenty years invited me to lecture at their Landscape School. The directors and curators of the many gardens I visited gave invaluable information and details. Finally, landscape architecture historians from across the world discussed gardens with me, especially Bill Tischler, Bill Mann, and Ruth Enis.

It is not possible to acknowledge by name all of the people who have contributed to this book. The students, docents and guides, and scholars with whom I have talked and worked, and whose ideas I have studied over the years were vitally important in the development stages and beyond. Many thanks to all who have supported me through this project.

—Miriam Easton Rutz

Slayton Arboretum. Photo by Douglas Coon, courtesy of Hillsdale College.

Afterword

Hidden Lake, Tipton. Photo by Balthazar Korab.

As we move into the twenty-first century gorgeous new gardens are being built in many of our cities and towns, and older gardens are being improved. Great gardens essentially maintain their original character, but they are always adapting to changes in usage and in plant material requirements. The gardens selected for this book are beautiful in all seasons of the year. They are basically barrier free and often have a garden shop with rest rooms. Many give tours. Some of these gardens require an entry fee, but most are open to the public all year long. This book is written for the citizens of Michigan and their guests, in hopes that it will increase their enjoyment and appreciation for the designs, details, flowers, and ambiance of these magnificent gardens in their historical contexts.